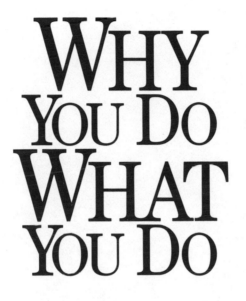

# WHY
## YOU DO
# WHAT
## YOU DO

# WHY YOU DO WHAT YOU DO

## BOBB BIEHL

THOMAS NELSON PUBLISHERS
Nashville

Published in Nashville, Tennessee, by Oliver-Nelson Books, a division of Thomas
Nelson, Inc., Publishers, and distributed in Canada by Word Communications,
Ltd., Richmond, British Columbia.

The Bible version used in this publication is THE NEW KING JAMES VERSION.
Copyright © 1979, 1980, 1982, Thomas Nelson, Inc., Publishers.

**Library of Congress Cataloging-in-Publication Data**

Biehl, Bobb.
    Why you do what you do / Bobb Biehl.
      p.    cm.
    ISBN 0-8407-9154-2 (hardcover)
    1. Emotions.   2. Affect (Psychology)  3. Self-defeating behavior.
  I. Title.
  BF561.B54   1993
  158'.1—dc20                                93–10149
                                                     CIP

Printed in the United States of America.

1 2 3 4 5 6 — 98 97 96 95 94 93

# Contents

Appendixes

# Special Appreciation

I would like to express my sincere appreciation to the wise men and women who have shared so freely of their wisdom and experiences in the design and development of the "why pattern," which explains why people do what they do.

Specifically, I would like to thank Steve Arterburn; Christy Artz; Karen Artz; Amy and Mike Bailey; Anne and Bob Batty; Dan Batty; Tricia and Allan Beeber; Bob Biehl, my father; Don Biehl; Barbara, Jim, Bonnie, and Debbie Blinn; Spencer Brand; Bill Broadwick; Kevin and Rita Caruso; George Caywood; Ward Coleman; Charles Debter; Georgie and Corky Eddins; John Erwin; Berry Fager; Jane and Terry Fleck; Ross Goebel; Ed Gruman; Robert Jeffress; Brian Johnson; Mary and Bruce Johnson; Susie Jones; Joe Kimbel; Patti and Mark Krone; Robert Lewis; Brad Lind; Bob and Kathleen

Lonac; Carol and George Madison; Marcus Maranto; Arlis Mathis; Debbie McCommons; Dottie and Josh McDowell; Gari and Bo Mitchell; Bob Nickel; Kimberly Parker; Linda and Dave Ray; Vickie and Joel Robertson; Claude Robold; Jamie Robold; Jann Saulsberry; Janet Showalter; Bob Smullin; Martha Staley; Rory Stark; Carol and Charles Thaxon; Bob Tiede; Ed Trenner; Glen Urquhart; Carol Walker; Steve Woodworth; David Wright; and Duane Zook.

# Introduction

How many times in the last twelve months have you asked yourself,

*Why* did I do that?

*Why* did that person threaten me?

*Why* did I try to intimidate him?

*Why* am I still so afraid of being rejected?

*Why* do I withdraw whenever I feel threatened?

*Why* am I a people pleaser?

*Why* am I such a perfectionist?

Or maybe you've asked, *Why* would someone who didn't need to shade the truth, stretch the truth, tell a white lie, or tell a bold, black gross lie? *Why* would someone do that?

Since 1976, I have spent approximately twelve days a month, usually ten hours a day (approximately 21,000 hours), behind the defenses of people, dealing with clients' "Why people do what they do questions":

- *Why* did my staff person lie?
- *Why* did my team leader explode when I asked a simple question?
- *Why* am I so tempted to sell my firm just when it has become extremely profitable?
- *Why* did my best vice president quit?

Bottom line . . . my life is spent answering the "why questions." My experience does not come as a professional writer, a psychologist, or a professor. My experience, as the president of a consulting firm called Masterplanning Group International, comes from dealing with very healthy, balanced, successful leaders who typically have many "why questions."

People seeking answers to the emotional mysteries of life come from all walks of life, including people making $100,000 a month, homemakers, pastors, presidents, people of all nationalities and races, females and males. They all wrestle at certain points with why they or others do what they do.

## The "Why Pattern"

A few years ago, I was walking on the beach and talking with a dearly loved and deeply troubled friend. As

2

we walked and shared where we were on our emotional pilgrimages, a very clear emotional pattern began to emerge that I had never seen before.

All of a sudden emotional mysteries that had stumped me for years in my own life were instantly solved! I went home and made careful notes on all of the questions and insights gained that hot summer afternoon along the beach in San Clemente, California.

In the next few months I drew my discovery on napkins, place mats, and legal pads for friends and clients. Universally, the response was overwhelmingly positive!

After sharing it with literally hundreds of people for hours and days at a time, I feel confident that it can be a great benefit to you. Thus, I've written about it in this book. The "why pattern" answers the age-old question: Why do people do what they do?

In its simplest form the "why pattern" looks like the diagram on the following page.

This "why pattern" applies to every person. Once clearly understood, the "why pattern" explains everything from fear of failure to unresolved relationships with parents in a logical, systematic, and practical way.

## A Step-by-Step Look at the "Why Pattern"

1. Every person has a *dominant childhood feeling* (e.g., blessed, ignored, or inadequate). This feeling (positive or negative) results in . . .

2. A *dominant adult phobia* (e.g., an unrealistic fear

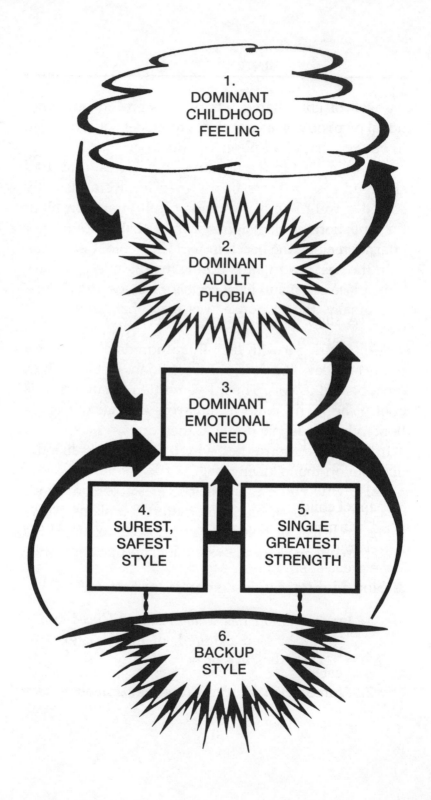

of failure, rejection, or insignificance). The phobia results in . . .

3. An adult *dominant emotional need* (e.g., to be accepted, loved, or recognized). To meet the dominant emotional need, you develop a . . .

4. *Surest, safest style* of relating to life (e.g., enabler, entertainer, or leader), which typically gets the need met. To meet the dominant emotional need, you also develop . . .

5. A *single greatest strength* (e.g., facilitating, persuading, or controlling). The combination of the single greatest strength and the surest, safest style meets the dominant emotional need as consistently as possible.

When your dominant emotional need is met, it temporarily reassures you that your dominant adult phobia is not real and that you will (*a*) never have to go back to the pain of childhood or (*b*) never have to leave the emotional warmth of the positive feelings of childhood. However, just in case your surest, safest style and your single greatest strength fail to get your dominant emotional need met, you also develop a . . .

6. *Backup style*, your negative dark side. In your backup style you combine your single greatest strength and your surest, safest style with force or pressure. You consider doing im-

moral, unethical, and even illegal things if necessary to have your dominant emotional need met. You use your backup style (e.g., cutting corners, workaholism, or withdrawing) to intimidate and manipulate people into meeting your dominant emotional need.

You can go to a doctor for a physical checkup, and the technician will put you in front of the sophisticated, expensive X ray equipment and you can see a fractured bone. But where do you go to get such a look at your emotions?

The "why pattern" is the tool. With it you will soon learn that a vast majority of your emotions can be explained in a logical way through understanding these six steps. This tool lets you see your emotions in a simple pattern—somewhat like seeing an X ray of your emotional system.

## The Three Selves

There is one catch, however, to all of this emotional mystery solving. Solving the emotional mysteries in your life takes reflection time.

You have to be willing to probe into your emotions far below the surface level into your heart of hearts. To explain what I mean, I need to draw a diagram I have used literally hundreds of times in my consultations.

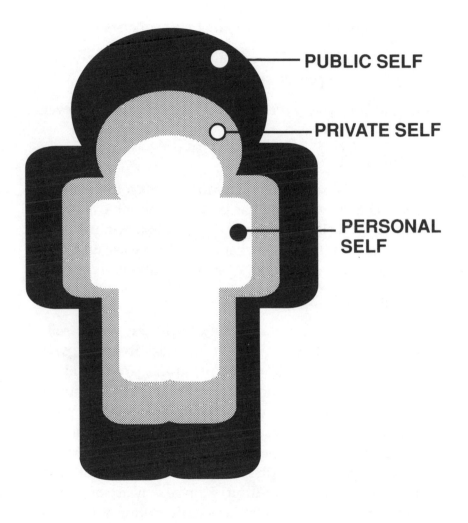

**PUBLIC SELF**

**PRIVATE SELF**

**PERSONAL
SELF**

Everyone has three selves.

1. You have a *public self* that everyone sees.

2. You have a *private self* that only close friends see in a private setting.

3. You have a *personal self* that only you have ever seen.

## Public Self

The public self is the one you try to keep polished. There is no flaw in it; it is as perfect as possible in every way. It's your image, your shell, your exterior, your social skin, your front. It's what other people see who just see you at church, at work, or on the street.

## Private Self

Then there is a second level of self, the private self. Your private self is made up of the roles that you play: mother or father, uncle or aunt, grandparent, and so on. It's the social relationships you have with relatives and friends who know you in the primary role you play.

You are known to them as mother or father, aunt or uncle, but they don't necessarily know you as a person. They call you by friendly, warm names like Aunt Karen or Uncle Phil, Grandma Kimbel or Strawberry Grandpa. But they aren't necessarily talking to the person. They are relating mostly role to role, mother to daughter, father to son, friend to friend.

## Personal Self

Finally, you have a personal self that no one has ever seen. Within this self you have thought things about yourself and other people that for whatever reason you have never cared to share or discuss with others.

You may have never had the opportunity to or never felt it was appropriate to. There may be a thousand reasons why you don't share what is inside. Nonetheless, there are certain things you have never told anyone.

When you have a heart-to-heart conversation with a dear and deeply trusted lifelong friend, you are actually exchanging glimpses into this third level of self. You are showing a part of you no one has yet seen and being given the same access to your friend's heart. You are having a heart-to-heart conversation.

# A Practical Conversation

This entire book is like a heart-to-heart chat. Because of the questions on these pages, you will think about very, very personal issues within a new framework that brings both objectivity and clarity.

And even though we are not actually sitting down for a chat before the fire on a quiet snowy night, I hope that together we can solve some of the emotional mysteries in the personal, confidential, protected, unheard part of your heart where you don't yet trust others to enter.

## Heart of Hearts Reflection

Several times in our conversation I'd like to suggest that you put the book down and in your heart of hearts reflect on the things you have just read. Typically, I will suggest that you reflect on one very specific question.

You may want to keep a journal marked with a fake title, something like "1969 Tax Records" so no one will bother it. Or as I have suggested to some, put your reflections in a locked box or someplace where no one will be tempted to "look" into your personal feelings.

Right now I would like to suggest that you get away by yourself for about thirty minutes to reflect on this question: What are the emotional mysteries in my heart?

What are the "why questions" you have never shared with anyone? Make an exhaustive list:

*Why* am I a people pleaser?

*Why* do I fear rejection?

*Why* do I need so desperately to be accepted?

*Why* do I withdraw under pressure?

*Why* do I choke in the ninth inning of life?

*Why* am I still afraid in the dark?

Once you can get them on paper, we can begin answering them one at a time. By the end of the book, you can have many, if not most, of your questions answered.

# A Solution to Emotional Mysteries

Right now you may be asking,

> Is it really worth the effort?
> Is it really worth the tears?
> Is it really worth the painful memories?

Solving emotional mysteries is like putting together a ten-thousand-piece picture puzzle—at times frustrating but pleasurable every time one of the ten thousand pieces finds its perfect home. You'll enjoy the journey!

Every single time you solve an emotional mystery, the best way to describe this feeling is pure pleasure. You are going to have a lot of pleasurable (puzzle-piece-fitting) experiences if you keep reading and interacting honestly with your "why pattern."

### Resolving Emotional Pain

Whenever there is a conflict, something I can't resolve or understand, an emotional mystery that remains a mystery, an inconsistency, a hurt, a confusion, it blocks my emotional growth, and it causes me emotional pain. I have found that the sense of emotional pain and confusion goes away only with the resolution and clarification of the answer to the question: Why did I, or they, do that?

## Caution: Don't carry your pain any longer. It isn't necessary!

One of the great pleasures of working on a book like this is imagining you reading it alone (in a study, at the beach, or by a quiet brook), crying gentle tears of pleasure and resolution, saying with relief, "Now I understand. Now it is okay. Now I don't ever have to deal with that emotional pain again."

At the same time a tremendous overwhelming sadness fills me when I think of people I've known who have carried emotional pain over a lifetime.

One woman who is now nearly seventy years old still carries the pain of a comment that her sister made when she was eleven years old. As a result, she has felt inadequate, resentful, and generally a second-class person . . . fifty-nine years of unnecessary emotional pain . . . pain that to her has been as real as a headache or backache.

*You do not have
to share your
personal thoughts,
fears, insights,
resolutions,
confusions,
or tears with anyone
until you are good
and ready!*

The possibility of helping you understand and re-solve some of your pain, and keeping you from carry-ing it around for a lifetime without the personal risk, expense, or embarrassment of talking to a psychologist, psychiatrist, or even a close friend, brings me great sat-isfaction. One of the major advantages of this book is that you can read it, interact with it, reflect on it, and resolve things without ever having to talk to another human being about it.

When certain issues in your life are resolved and clear, you are obviously free to share any of them with some of your dearest, most trusted friends. Having a close friend walk with you on the beach and being able to tell that person about some of the things you've seen, understood, and resolved that are no longer painful to you or are now crystal clear in your thinking can be very pleasurable.

But you don't have to share one single word until you're ready. This sharing point may never come, but it may come much sooner than you think. Whether or not you share what you experience is 100 percent in your control.

## Results of Understanding

There are about ten really helpful results of understanding why you do what you do at a far deeper level:

1. *Accepting yourself and others,* not feeling other people's emotional blowups or your own fears as painfully

2. *Communicating more intimately* with your spouse, children, parents, and other dear friends

3. *Counseling more effectively* with loved ones and friends in emotional confusion and pain

4. *Mentoring, teaching, and coaching more successfully* with new depths of understanding of why people do what they do

5. *Preventing the passing of the pain of your past* to your children and grandchildren

6. *Protecting and/or monitoring your need level* as a preventative against such things as manipulation, vulnerability, workaholism, perfectionism, and feeling emotionally driven

7. *Resolving strained, troubled, or painful relationships* with parents, siblings, and friends from childhood and in adulthood

8. *Selecting the right pastors, presidents, and other key staff members,* saving enormous amounts of wasted time, energy, and money because of one unwise decision

9. *Solving painful emotional mysteries,* freeing you to once again start growing toward full emotional maturity . . . away from your dominant adult phobia of failure, rejection, or authority figures

10. *Understanding what others need from you,* understanding why they need it and the lengths to which they will go to meet the need

## Aha!

When I teach seminars for Dave Ray in Detroit, Michigan, he encourages students to say "aha!" aloud each time they see something or resolve something for the first time.

When you have an "aha!" experience as you read through this book, write "aha!" in the margin. That will help you see and feel the progress you're making.

Sometime, I would enjoy hearing how many "aha!" experiences you have. Your experiences make the hundreds of hours that go into a book like this worthwhile.

Chapter 1

---

# What Was Your Dominant Childhood Feeling?

*Every child has a dominant childhood feeling that results
in a predictable emotional-motivational
pattern in adulthood.*

## The Most Fundamental Shaping
## of Your Adult Attitudes and
## Styles Is Actually Done
## Before You're a Teenager

In our teen-twenties-oriented culture, a lot of people assume that what happens in the teenage years has the most influence in shaping the adult years. However, the more I listen to adult executives and get into why they're doing what they're doing, the more I see the dramatic, predictable parallels between preteen years and adult behavior.

The feelings you had as a child were neither good nor

bad, right nor wrong, accurate nor inaccurate. They were simply how you felt. You cannot help how you felt. You can help how you act or react to the feelings as an adult. So don't hesitate or feel embarrassed to say, "As a child, the dominant feeling I can remember having was feeling _____."

As an adult, you may conclude there may, or may not, have been a reality-based cause for you to have that feeling. Maybe you felt as a child that your parents didn't love you, but as an adult, you see that they really did. Maybe they desperately loved you, but if you *felt* unloved, all of your emotional development was based on the assumption that you were unloved.

Whether or not you had a logical reason for feeling as you did as a child, you need to identify how you actually felt and then decide, as an adult with adult eyes, if it was logical, real, harmful, or not harmful.

For example, when I was five or six years old, I would go to my paternal grandparents' house for meals, and my grandfather would always do a predictable thing. I would get right in the middle of corn on the cob, bean soup, or dark chocolate cake, and my grandfather would look over at me, in front of everyone, and ask in a very serious voice: "Are you going to pay for this meal?"

I never knew what to say. I knew I didn't have any money. I thought he must be kidding, but what if he weren't? And I didn't think anyone else had to pay. It made me feel like crying. He didn't smile, but everyone else laughed. After he played the game a few times, I

19

felt my grandfather didn't like me because he was making me feel so bad.

As an adult with adult eyes, I see clearly that he really liked me and that was his way of teasing. But as a child, I didn't understand. So when I was with my paternal grandfather, I always felt uncomfortable, ill at ease. I felt that I didn't fit, I didn't belong, I wasn't acceptable to him.

Well, those were childhood feelings. I have to say that those were *real feelings* as a child. The other reality was that he liked me as much as any of his fifty-two grandchildren. It wasn't that he was against me or didn't like me, but the feeling I had was based on his form of humor.

Whatever your feeling was, whether it was good, bad, or indifferent, recognize the feeling and then just ask, What did that mean? Did it really affect me for life, or was it just something I felt as a child? Again, see each childhood feeling as a piece of the puzzle.

## One Key in Understanding Your "Why Pattern" Is Identifying Your Emotionally Loaded Words, Phrases, or Actions

**Emotionally loaded *means that these words, phrases, or actions make your emotional system react in a major way.***

For example, let's say you're attached to a lie detector and the monitoring person speaks ten words. The lie detector monitors all of your impulses electronically with a needle that goes back and forth. You can hear nine of those words, and the needle may vary only one-sixteenth of an inch. But on the tenth word the telltale arm swings rapidly five to ten inches indicating that the word was emotionally loaded!

That's because your autonomic nervous system, which you don't even control, has this emotional reaction to the word—like *accepted, rejected, incompetent,* or *failure.* Whatever the word, it causes an emotional reaction you feel but cannot consciously control.

Part of what this book is about is helping you identify those emotionally loaded words, phrases, or actions and then figure out what they mean: How does my emotional system work? What triggers it? Why does it act and react as it does? What are the emotionally loaded words and phrases that trigger me? Why do they cause that reaction?

For example, I'll never forget that one of my extremely competent clients told me her mother says to her every once in a while in a soft, sad, slow voice, "Oh, honey, let me do it." She said, "When I hear that phrase, every cell in my body wants to scream because I know exactly what that means emotionally. It means, 'You're incompetent. Let Mommy do it.' I'm thirty-five years old, and my mother still looks at me as incompetent. And she communicates this to me with the same

21

phrase she communicated it to me thirty years ago: 'Oh, honey, let me do it.'"

There may be an emotionally loaded gesture or look. One male executive told me that his dad had a look he would give him, and that look meant, "You're doing it wrong; you're incompetent." He said, "That one look told me everything."

---

One word of caution: Each chapter presents emotionally loaded words and phrases for you to explore. When I first started asking people to identify the dominant childhood feeling, the most typical response was, "Could you give me some examples of what you mean?"

These comments by others are meant to stimulate your memory, not limit your options. Your dominant childhood feeling is best understood and most easily remembered in your own word or words. Feel 100 percent free to take any of the words that other people have used and adapt them as much as you like! For example, someone else may have said, "Afraid and fearful." You may add, "Of Uncle Zebo."

---

Everyone wants to be loved, accepted, and appreciated, but not everyone has the same emotionally loaded

feelings attached to these words. Being accepted socially does not mean the same thing (is not equally
emotionally loaded) to everyone. It may not mean to
you what it means to your spouse. It may not mean to
you what it does to your children or grandchildren.
Let's find your emotionally loaded words.

## Notes

1. In the dominant childhood feeling section, you
are determining how you felt as a child. You are *not* trying to clarify how you feel today about your childhood.
(See chart following).

2. The specific age you choose to focus on may vary
a great deal from what someone else may choose. It de-
pends on the age you feel was the strongest influence in
shaping your adult "why pattern."

3. Your dominant childhood feeling is the key to understanding the entire content of this book and the
book's application to your life.

Take your time. Change any answer you like. Reflect
as much as necessary to develop a crystal clear understanding of your dominant childhood feeling.

There are eight dominant childhood feeling categories. Please rate the following items on a scale of 1 to 10:

   1 = not emotionally loaded for me
      (no emotional reaction)

   10 = emotionally loaded in a major way for me
       (major emotional reaction)

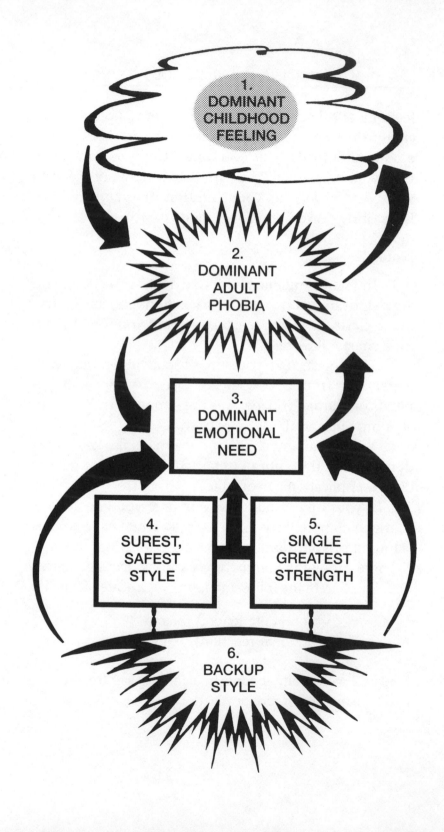

Feel free to adapt the words and phrases on the following pages to more accurately express your feelings. Add; cross out; modify. Make notes in the margins.

You may want to use a pencil. You may want to change your ratings several times over the next few days. Your changes are no problem.

As a child (preteen), my dominant childhood feeling was that of being . . .

1. _____ *conditionally loved* or inconsistently loved or unloved.

   - Desperately wanted to please; hyperconscientious
   - Performance driven; striving for approval; unable to do enough (to be really loved)
   - Unbonded; unconnected; unwanted
   - Unpredictably loved *and* criticized, scolded, or abused
   - Other

   _____

2. _____ *destined*, blessed, chosen, special, or loved.

   - Accepted; secure; protected
   - Felt confident as a child
   - Gifted mentally, physically, spiritually, etc.
   - Loved unconditionally; free to explore widely—I

felt there was nothing I couldn't do if I decided to!
- Told by adults I was blessed, a special child
- Other

_____

3. _____ *favored* by adults over peers.

- Admired as (group, team, family) hero
- Adored; preferred by adults over my peers
- Treated as Daddy's "princess" or Mommy's "little man"
- Other

_____

4. _____ *ignored emotionally,* unimportant, un-needed, unnoticed.

- Became a lonesome child behind an "I'm okay" mask
- Competed for attention and/or affection; never felt special
- Stuck in the middle; lost in all of the kids
- Other

_____

5. _____ *inadequate* to meet expectations.

- Cared for the family; replaced a deceased parent—"now the mommy"; protected siblings from abusive parent(s)
- Compared myself with others—they always win
- Felt stupid, awkward, or ugly compared to sibling(s)
- Picked on frequently by other kids
- Subjected to negative comments about physical features
- Unable to do "right things right" for emotionally explosive parent
- Unable to protect myself from adult offenders
- Other

_____

6. _____ *insecure*, unsafe, or vulnerable.

- Abandonment—death of parent(s) or divorce
- Abuse—one parent physically abusive of the other, parents fighting verbally a lot
- Alcoholism—parent(s) drank a lot
- Disability—parent(s) disabled or vulnerable
- Instability—unpredictable environment, lots of tension, "like walking on eggshells"
- Poverty—constant threat of hunger, eviction, etc.

- Trauma—child abuse, incest, or rape
- Other

_____

7. _____ *intimidated* or dominated by a person(s).

- By extended family member(s)
- By father or mother
- By older siblings
- By peers
- By other(s)

_____

8. _____ *unacceptable socially* to my peers.

- Embarrassed by family style, name, or reputation
- Embarrassed by father or mother
- Maintained false social-emotional mask
- Moved a lot; never really fit
- Never accepted by peers; was a loner
- Never learned sports
- Other

_____

Of the eight dominant childhood feeling categories, the one I felt the most strongly was

1. _____ *conditionally loved* or inconsistently loved or unloved.
2. _____ *destined,* blessed, chosen, special, or loved.
3. _____ *favored* by adults over peers.
4. _____ *ignored emotionally,* unimportant, un-needed, or unnoticed.
5. _____ *inadequate* to meet expectations.
6. _____ *insecure,* unsafe, or vulnerable.
7. _____ *intimidated* or dominated by a person(s).
8. _____ *unacceptable socially* to my peers.

The way I would put this feeling into my own words would be: As a child, my dominant childhood feeling was that of _____

_____.

Many people have trouble remembering childhood. If you have trouble, it may help you to complete the following sentence:

As a child, I'll never forget feeling _____

_____.

Often, horrible memories are completely blocked out. I wouldn't try too hard, without professional help, to remember any of those memories. If it's blocked out, leave it blocked out unless you decide that it's hurting you enough to need to seek professional help.

A word of caution: Be careful about assuming negative consequences when you can't remember clearly. A small percentage of professional counselors and well-meaning friends give the impression that being unable to remember means you were molested as a child.

# If you can't remember your childhood feelings, don't panic!

That is *not* automatically true. You may have had to deal with some hard things but don't jump to conclusions about what they were.

## Dominant Childhood Feelings Can Be Positive and/or Negative

As you read the book, if your dominant childhood feeling was positive, you may ask, "Did some people really have extremely negative childhood feelings?" Or if your dominant childhood feeling was very negative, you may ask, "Did some people really have extremely positive childhood feelings?"

You may be surprised to learn that some people had nearly ideal childhoods; they can remember no negative feelings. At the same time some have generally negative memories. And some remember only traumatically negative emotions.

If individuals had a negative childhood, they don't ever want to experience those negative feelings again. So they live their adult lives to get away or keep away from feeling the negative childhood feelings. But if individuals had a positive childhood, they want to be assured in adult life that what they're experiencing confirms that they never have to leave the emotional warmth of those childhood memories. Don't assume that every child experienced what you did, positively or negatively.

A lot of people had what they refer to as a "Leave It to Beaver" childhood. They can't think of any negatives. It was all very positive. They had friends, they had financial security, and their parents stayed married. It was a very, very affirming, wonderful, warm, positive childhood.

There is no such thing as a perfect parent, but there are a lot of very healthy parents! A lot of parents gave their children balance. A lot of parents were very positive, with a very strong way of affirming, and it beget in the children a certain amount of life confidence that other people did not get and do not have without a great deal of effort.

If you had ideal parents, don't spend all your time trying to figure out where your parents were wrong or what they did wrong or how negatively they affected you if, in fact, they were positive influences in your life.

---

## How do you see your childhood?

☐ *Really positive*
☐ *Sort of positive*
☐ *Sort of negative*
☐ *Traumatically negative*

---

## Most People Have a Single Dominant Childhood Feeling

As you looked back and tried to identify your dominant childhood feeling, you may have had some mixed feelings. For example, you were loved by one parent and rejected by another. Frequently, a child is favored by one parent and receives a lot of pressure (or abuse) from the other parent. In that case, follow both patterns through. Ask yourself, How did I feel as the favored child? How did I feel as the rejected child?

You may find that you have two "why patterns," and each dominant childhood feeling results in its own dominant adult phobia and dominant emotional need and so on. You will have two "why patterns" when we get to chapter 7 and see how all of the pieces fit together.

If more than two of the eight categories were heavily emotionally loaded for you, if you felt destined, inadequate, insecure, intimidated, unacceptable, and unloved, chances are, professional counseling would be helpful at some point along the way.

If you have four or more dominant childhood feelings, you likely have a complicated personality. If you have five dominant childhood feelings, five dominant adult phobias, and so on, you have a very complicated personality.

Most people tend to have one dominant childhood feeling and another one or two that were important but not necessarily dominant.

## An Interesting Variation

Many people felt one way with adults (e.g., favored) and a totally different way with their peers (e.g., unacceptable). They may have felt very, very accepted by adults in their lives—Mama's girl or Daddy's girl, or Daddy's boy or Mama's boy—but with their friends they were not accepted.

I call this a split. You divide your world into two parts: the part that relates to adults (people who are

33

substantially older than you) and the part that relates to peers (those who are your own age).

Split patterns may be almost totally different patterns. A split does not mean you are schizophrenic or have two personalities; it simply means you have different ways of relating to different people.

*The same concept of a split may be true between what you needed from your mother and what you needed from your father.*

The way you related to your mother when you were a child is typically the way you relate to older women today. And the way you related to your father is likely your most comfortable way to relate to older men. So with the older women you relate to, you may have a very distinct reaction to those who parallel your mother, whereas you may have a totally different reaction to older men.

For example, if your mother treated you tenderly and your father treated you harshly, you will tend to expect all older women to treat you tenderly and all older men to treat you harshly.

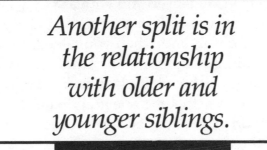

*Another split is in the relationship with older and younger siblings.*

Let's say you had an older brother or sister who watched out for you, and you had a younger brother and sister you watched out for. As you relate to older friends versus younger friends today, you may relate to them very differently. You may try to protect those who seem younger than you, and you may assume that your older friends are there to watch out for you.

You may be five years apart or two years apart or even the same age. But if you *perceive* someone to be like your older brother or like your younger sister, your tendency will be to relate to the person the way you did to your older or younger sibling.

# Who Were the Emotionally Significant People in Your Childhood?

Perhaps you grew up with four grandparents, but only one of them was emotionally significant. You felt that one grandparent saw the real you. That grandparent saw you as special, bonded with you, listened to you as a person, and loved you with a special love. The other three saw you as just another kid. They felt no special love for you, and when you talked, they heard what you said but didn't really understand all you meant to say. As you look back at your childhood with adult eyes, you see that the one grandparent was emotionally important in your development as a person and the other three were not. They were there, and they were important as grandparents but were not emotionally significant.

You could have had fifteen aunts and uncles, but only one of them was emotionally significant. You could have played a lot with five or ten friends, but only two of them were emotionally significant. Those were the people you let see your heart (your personal self), and they let you see theirs. You had a *relationship* with them; you could talk heart-to-heart on very special occasions.

Who were the emotionally significant people in your childhood? Make a list. Those relationships were the bases on which you formed your opinions of what relationships were supposed to be and what roles were supposed to be played.

If your emotionally significant relationships are not clear, you may want to ask yourself,

> How did I *feel* when I was with Dad?
>
> How did I *feel* when I was with Mom?
>
> How did I *feel* when I was with my younger sister?
>
> How did they make me *feel*?
>
> Did they make me *feel* better, worse, less, inferior, or superior?

# *Heart of Hearts Reflection*

You might want to take some time now and reflect on those relationships and how you felt about each of them.

Ask yourself, How did I feel about Aunt Lois or Uncle Wayne? How did I actually feel about various people in my childhood? Did I have *any* feelings toward them?

They saw me physically, but did they interact with me emotionally? Did they seem to care whether I existed? Was I something to be put up with, or was I a special person?

Take an hour and go for a walk right now *if possible,* and just think about each of the people in your childhood. You may be very surprised when you answer the question: Who were the emotionally significant people of my childhood?

---

You may say, "You know, I've just gotten back from my one-hour walk, and I can't identify anyone. There was no one I felt was really emotionally significant to me. I just felt like no one really cared whether I lived or died. My entire childhood felt emotionally detached. No one seemed to pay any attention."

This feeling of having been totally ignored relationally is far more common than you can imagine. You will find chapters 8, 9, and 10 especially helpful.

Another way to look at this emotionally significant question is to ask, Who did I desperately want to please?

Who did you want to approve of what you were doing? Who were you most trying to please by your clothing, hairstyle, attitudes, and so on? The answer is frequently a defining reflection in terms of emotionally significant influences in childhood. You may not have felt bonded to those people, but they significantly influenced your values.

# A Child's Perception of Childhood Is Far More Shaping Than the Realities

We lived in South Bend, Indiana, when our daughter, Kimberly, and our son, J. Ira, were young. Since those early days, we have lived in southern California. When the children were old enough to appreciate it and young enough to still want to go, we took two automobile trips around the United States, visiting clients and family for the summer.

On one trip, we decided to go back and visit our very first home in South Bend, Indiana. About fifty miles west of South Bend we began talking about that house. Kimberly, who was six years old when we left South Bend, was then eleven years old. We started asking her to describe what our house was like.

To give you some perspective, our California house was about 2,500 square feet, on about one-half acre of ground, with three bedrooms and two and a half baths, and the house in South Bend was 1,100 square feet.

So we asked Kimberly, "How would you describe our house in South Bend compared to the house in California?"

She said, "Oh, they were about the same size, but the South Bend house is probably a little bigger."

We asked, "How big was your bedroom compared to the one you have now?"

She said, "Oh, my South Bend bedroom was quite a bit bigger."

In reality, it was a ten-by-eleven-foot room, and her California bedroom was a twelve-by-fourteen-foot room. We went on and on, and in every dimension, to her childhood eyes, the small South Bend house was "just huge." When we lived there, she was a little person in a big house.

## *Perceptions are more shaping than realities.*

Some people grew up poor, but they didn't know it. I'll never forget watching Dolly Parton, the country music singer, being interviewed on television, and she said, "We grew up poor, but my mama never let us know we were poor." She didn't feel emotionally burned by being poor. But I have a client who said, "I grew up poor and felt poor and embarrassed, and I still feel all that." He is emotionally *driven* to eliminate the possibility of becoming poor again, with cash reserves and more cash reserves, and cash reserves in other countries, and new companies and different companies. There's never enough because of his *perception*

40

(dominant childhood feeling) of being poor and insecure as a child.

## Every Child Starts Out a Love Sponge

Can you name people who unconditionally loved
you in your childhood? Every child needs at least one
person who loves without conditions. A parent, a
grandparent, an aunt or uncle, a friend, or a neighbor
can communicate to the child, "You are worthy of love,
you are worthy of adult attention, you are worthy of my
love, and you get it regardless of what you *do* or *do not
do*." This unconditional love gives the child a sense of
self-worth.

*Consider being
a "love giver"
for children who
appear to feel
unloved today!*

But if as an adult you look everywhere in your childhood and find no unconditional love, that's when the
adult question comes, Am I worthy of love at all? You

41

obviously are worthy of being loved just because you are a human being, but you may not feel like it at times.

If you did not get unconditional love as a child, you will seek it for a lifetime and will do nearly anything to receive it.

Every child needs unconditional love, even the child who seems least likely to respond—the one with the behavior problem, the one who seems the coldest, the most aloof, the most reserved, the most stoic. That child needs love as much as the child who is cuddling next to you. *Assume that children are love sponges.*

When you give a little bit of love to a cold, aloof, unresponsive child who has had no love at all, it's just like putting water on a dry sponge. The water may sit on the surface and not appear to sink in at all. But when you continue putting water on the dry sponge, sooner or later it begins to sink in, and then it sinks in more and more and more and more.

But don't stop loving a child who appears not to be accepting the love. The reality is that the child does not know how to accept it. He desperately needs it, like a dry sponge needs water, but he may not know how to absorb it properly.

Continue to be patient, loving, and accepting. Continue telling her that you love her regardless of what she does or doesn't do. Point out the things that she's done right. Sooner or later the child will be able to absorb it.

Once he develops an ability to absorb love, he'll tend to want to get close to you physically and be with you because children need constant love.

If you didn't get love as a child, where have you found it as an adult? If you never had it as a child, you're probably reluctant to accept that you are worthy of love without performance—whether it is the love of God or the love of a spouse.

Your parents may have communicated, "You're lovable *if* . . . ," or "You're lovable, *but* . . . ," or "You're lovable *and* keep practicing."

But was there someone in your life who communicated by actions if not by words, "You're lovable just because I love you, you're okay just the way you are, and you don't have to be something you're not"? That person was influential in your life, whether or not you spent a lot of time with the individual.

> *A child who felt no love in childhood had a traumatic childhood even if there was no single trauma.*

I've talked to adults who had a very traumatic childhood because at no time can they remember being

43

loved just because they were who they were. Small children may not *feel* loved if they are not *told* they are loved in words.

Again, tell children you love them! For the children you truly love,

- *tell* and show them you love them.
- *tell* them what they do right.
- *tell* them when they are creative.
- *tell* them they are loving.
- *tell* them they are special.

Recognize their strengths. The words you use to tell the children what you see in them help to shape the self-concept at a very early age.

Chapter 2

---

# What Is Your Dominant Adult Phobia?

*A dominant childhood feeling leads to a dominant adult phobia*
*(e.g., fear of failure, rejection, or insignificance).*

Your dominant adult phobia is the unrealistic fear that you will be forever trapped in the fears of your childhood or, if you have positive childhood feelings, you will lose the emotional warmth of your childhood as you become an adult!

There are eight dominant adult phobia categories. Please rate the following items on a scale of 1 to 10:

1 = not emotionally loaded for me

10 = very emotionally loaded for me

Remember, you are free to make any changes you like.

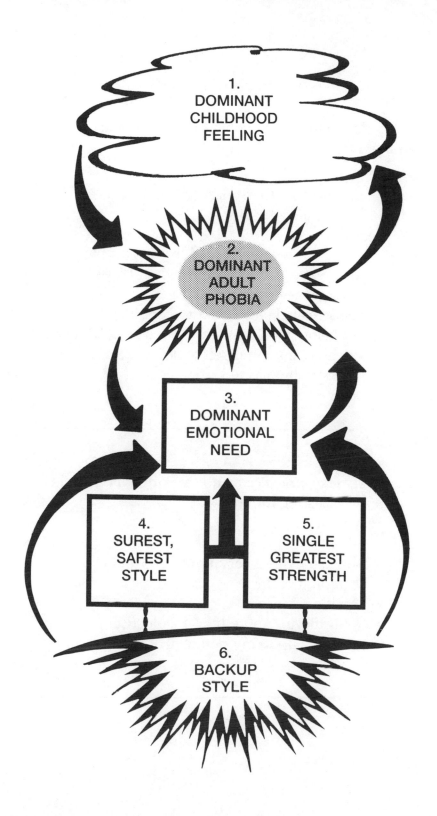

My dominant adult phobia (unrealistic fear) is in the area of . . .

1. _____ *rejection* (personal) (emotional focus: I am unloved).
     Fear of . . .

   • Losing affection of an individual I love
   • Never achieving intimacy
   • Never really being loved unconditionally
   • Not being good enough to be worthy of love
   • Revealing my inner self to someone, then being personally rejected
   • Other

   _____

2. _____ *insignificance* or not making a noticeable or lasting difference.
     Fear of . . .

   • Being stuck in a very limited position
   • Dying in obscurity
   • Leaving no legacy
   • Not achieving more than mediocrity
   • Not living up to my potential or my expectations
   • Other

   _____

3. _____ *failure* to keep a favored position.
Fear of . . .

- Disappointing those who count on me or look up to me
- Losing admiration; being rejected by my group
- Losing (family, group, team) "hero" status
- Not being recognized or respected as the "hero" of the group I am leading
- Not being reelected
- Other

---

4. _____ *invisibility,* being ignored, unnoticed, or unseen.
Fear of . . .

- Being a wallflower
- Being alone, isolated
- Being expendable, unneeded, or unimportant
- Being forgotten, out of the "mainstream," off the track
- Not being taken seriously
- Not getting people to listen to me
- Other

---

5. _____ *failure* to feel personally adequate because of
    poor performance.
   Fear of . . .

   - Appearing "dumb," "stupid," "slow," or "in-
     competent"
   - Being discovered—maybe I don't "have it"
   - Doing it wrong; not doing it right
   - Failing to meet expectations
   - Others' seeing the faults I try to cover up
   - Other

   _____

6. _____ *dependence* and then being abandoned or let
    down.
   Fear of . . .

   - Being controlled or trapped emotionally
   - Being deceived; trusting people too far
   - Being poor; not being able to maintain a comfort-
     able life-style
   - Losing control; not being able to take care of my-
     self
   - Other

   _____

7. _____ *failure* to be seen as an adult.
   Fear of . . .

   - Being second-string, not in their league
   - Dealing with authority figures—dominant men
     or women
   - Facing harsh men or women
   - Not being seen as a "mature woman" or a "real
     man"
   - Not being taken seriously (listened to) as an
     adult
   - Other

8. _____ *rejection* (social) (emotional focus: the group
            has rejected me).
   Fear of . . .

   - Being rejected by peers
   - Feeling the disapproval of others
   - Looking foolish in front of my peers
   - Not being accepted socially
   - Not being well liked
   - Not being popular or liked by my friends
   - Other

Of the eight dominant adult phobias (unrealistic fears), the one I personally struggle with is a phobia in the area of

1. _____ *rejection* (personal) (I am unloved).
2. _____ *insignificance* or not making a noticeable or lasting difference.
3. _____ *failure* to keep a favored position.
4. _____ *invisibility,* being ignored, unnoticed, or unseen.
5. _____ *failure* to feel personally adequate because of poor performance.
6. _____ *dependence* and then being abandoned or let down.
7. _____ *failure* to be seen as an adult.
8. _____ *rejection* (social) (the group has rejected me).

The way I would put this phobia into my own words would be: As an adult, I frequently have an unrealistic fear of _____

_____.

What if you can't think of any phobia? What is your worst nightmare? What is the thing you dread someday may happen? It may not have ever happened to you, but it's the thing you dread the most. What kind of situations make you the most uneasy?

If you had a dominantly positive childhood, the fear is frequently that you will never be able to return to or keep the favored position of childhood. It's the fear of losing the position of being the favored child or of not realizing your true destiny.

## Dominant Adult Phobias Are Extremely Frustrating Because from Other People's Perspective, There Is No Visible (Real) Basis for the Fear

Consider a beauty contestant who feels she is a fat little girl or is going to be a fat person, or she thinks of herself as a fat person because she was a chubby child. Fear of being overweight is her dominant adult phobia.

The fear is not realistic. It has no objective reality. When friends hear that she's afraid she's too fat, they say, "Are you kidding?"

But your phobia is just as surprising to other people. You may be afraid of being controlled, you may be afraid of disappointing someone, or you may be afraid of insignificance. When you tell your best friend your phobia, the person responds, "Are you kidding?" What the person doesn't see initially is that many of your adult patterns are reactions to the phobia.

So, phobias are very real to us, but most of them don't match the facts of adult life. They're simply the result of a dominant childhood feeling.

53

For example, one time we were buying a house. We had put money down on the house and were planning to move to a great little community. It was a nicer house and lot than we had in the community where we were then living, and we had interacted with the people in the area and liked them.

## *Dominant adult phobias are unpredictable and, at times, very embarrassing.*

All of a sudden I had a severe reaction that I didn't understand. I just wanted out of there. With everything within me I wanted out. We left that little town and *never* went back.

Fifteen years later, as I was working on my "why pattern," it became obvious to me why I had such an unreasonable reaction to that situation. I was afraid—my dominant adult phobia was causing me to have a major overreaction.

Some dominant adult phobias coming out of childhood can be drastically reduced once the *cause* of the phobia can be looked at with adult eyes.

# The Dominant Adult Phobia Is the Single Hardest Area in Which to Trust God and Other People

Many spiritually mature Christian leaders say, "I pray and I pray and I pray, and letting go of the fear of being rejected or disappointing someone or leaving the fear of insignificance up to God seems just about impossible!" Spiritual answers to phobias don't always seem to bring reassurance to a person. In other areas the same person may have great faith.

Trusting people in the area of your phobia is also extremely difficult. Your closest friend may have proven her love time and time again, but if your dominant adult phobia is a fear of being rejected personally, you may be reluctant to trust her.

A common pattern I've seen is one that combines a fear of people and a fear of God. For example, if your human father abandoned you, you have a phobia of being abandoned by everyone else, including God. The fact that God loves you unconditionally is an almost impossible truth to accept emotionally, even for a pastor who preaches sermons on the unconditional love and grace of God.

The best way I know to grow in the dominant adult phobia area is to memorize and then meditate on rational, dependable, adult truth. As you reflect on these truths, your mind can begin to be renewed into a new

55

adult view. But it doesn't happen quickly or easily. (See Appendix 1:13. "Meditation and Memory.")

## Perhaps the Most Common Dominant Adult Phobia Is the Fear of Failure

Many people have a phobia in the area of failure, even though everything they've done to this point—in elementary school, junior high, high school, college, and adulthood—has been successful.

*Failure means three very different things to people.*

1. FEAR OF FAILURE = LOSS OF FAVORED PO-SITION
   "If I fail, people won't admire me anymore, and I will no longer be the hero."

2. FEAR OF FAILURE = FEELING OF PER-SONAL INADEQUACY BECAUSE OF POOR PERFORMANCE
   "If I fail, I will feel personally inadequate again. I have failed to meet other people's ex-

pectations of me. I am an inadequate person."

3. FEAR OF FAILURE = FEAR OF NOT BEING RESPECTED AS AN ADULT
   "If I fail, I guess it proves that I am not a 'real man' [or a 'mature woman'] after all. No wonder people treat me like a kid. I'm no adult."

> *No emotionally healthy human wants to fail, but that is different from having a dominant adult phobia in the area of failure!*

To some people, the word *failure* is a very, very heavily emotionally loaded word. It is a dominant adult phobia.

As for me, I don't want to fail, I have no interest in failing, I don't like to fail, but it isn't a phobia of mine, either. I don't go around thinking, *Am I going to fail?* I never worry about that. I basically assume that sooner or later I'm going to succeed. I certainly have phobias like everyone, but failure is not one of them.

> # *The dominant adult phobia in the area of failure is often tied to the emotional mask.*

When you put on an emotional mask (an emotional "false front") early in childhood, you typically have a tremendous fear of failure because it may lead to your exposure. You're afraid that you look like an adult, but if you fail, you're going to be exposed as a child in an adult's body.

Therefore, you become defensive, overcontrolling, and nonrelational. You keep your mask snugly in place because you don't want anyone to see that you are emotionally a six-year-old child. So you don't ever expose how you really feel about anything.

The emotional mask stays in place:

> I'm tough!
>
> Everything is okay!
>
> You can't hurt me!
>
> I've got everything under control!

The mask is typically a protection from exposing a fear of failing and being rejected. Typically, even your closest friends are not allowed behind your emotional mask. (See Appendix 1:6. "Emotional Masks.")

# Heart of Hearts Reflection

What is your dominant adult phobia? Trace it back to your childhood. What instances contributed to the development of this phobia? What is the truth about this area as you now look at it with adult eyes?

What are the adult truths, Scripture verses, quotes, and realities you can memorize or carry with you to read to help you keep a more reality-based perspective in this area?

Chapter 3

---

# What Is Your Dominant Emotional Need?

*A combination of your dominant childhood feeling and
your dominant adult phobia results in a dominant
emotional need in adulthood (e.g., need
to be loved, respected, or accepted).*

Pinpointing a dominant emotional need fundamentally answers the question: Why do I do what I do?

There are eight basic adult dominant emotional needs. Please rate the following items on a scale of 1 to 10:

1 = not emotionally loaded for me

10 = very emotionally loaded for me

Remember, you are free to make any changes you like!

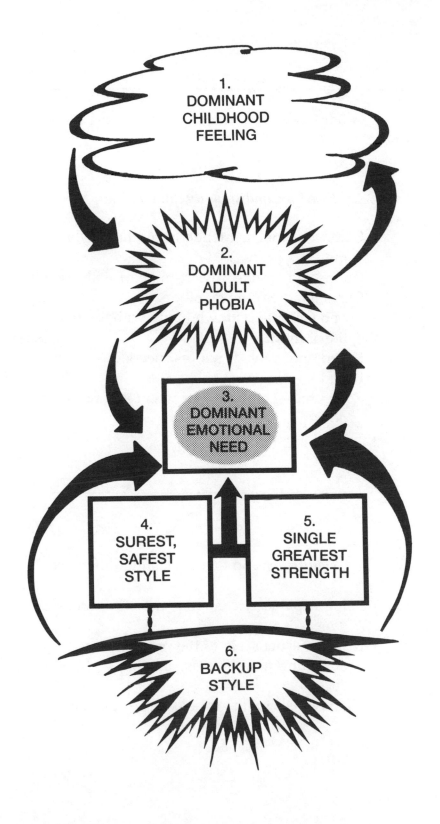

As an adult, I have a dominant emotional need to be . . .

1. _____ *loved unconditionally,* just as I am.

- Cared for; touched tenderly by those who love me
- Connected, bonded, heart-to-heart with friends
- Considered worthy by others
- Loved (accepted) for who I am without an emotional mask
- Loved and wanted, not just needed
- Loved, even when I fail
- Reassured—I am loved for who I am, not what I do
- Special to someone
- Other

2. _____ *significant* and make a lasting difference.

- Being a pioneer; changing the way things are done
- Being indispensable to the program
- Establishing new records; making a big difference
- Gaining recognition as a leader or pioneer

- Obtaining respect from peers for my significant contribution
- Other

_____

3. _____ *admired* as (group, team, family) "hero."

- Honored as outstanding, above and beyond my peers
- Looked up to as a "hero"
- Noticed as the person who "really made it happen"
- Praised by my peers
- Other

_____

4. _____ *recognized*, not ignored.

- Called by my name, not a nickname (for that instant I feel the very center of the speaker's attention)
- Listened to; my opinions considered seriously, clearly understood
- Spotlighted!
- Thought of constantly as needed and important
- Other

_____

5. _____ *appreciated* for a job well done.

- Appreciated and/or rewarded for what I do right
- Needed by people, especially by the really needy
- Sent appreciation notes; appreciation goes a long way, far beyond just money
- Told "Great job . . . thank you!" (tells me I was adequate for this situation)
- Other

_____

6. _____ *secure* and in control.

- Financially secure; cash strong with major reserves
- Powerful; protected
- Safe; not needing to depend on others
- Socially safe and appropriate
- Tenured at work; seniority
- Other

_____

7. _____ *respected* as an adult, equal to other adults.

- Considered competent
- Respected as a person

- Respected for my ability
- Respected for my expertise
- Trusted
- Other

---

8. _____ *accepted socially,* included and invited socially with freedom to be who I really am.

- Accepted by the group; included in their plans
- Approved of by the team
- Invited to join, to attend, to belong
- Liked by everyone . . . loved by a few
- Other

---

Of the eight adult dominant emotional needs, the
one I personally need the very most and with the deep-
est emotion is the need to be

1. _____ *loved unconditionally,* just as I am.
2. _____ *significant* and make a lasting difference.
3. _____ *admired* as (group, team, family) "hero."
4. _____ *recognized,* not ignored.
5. _____ *appreciated* for a job well done.
6. _____ *secure* and in control.

7. _____ *respected* as an adult, equal to other adults.
8. _____ *accepted socially,* included and invited socially with freedom to be who I really am.

The way I would put this dominant emotional need into my own words would be: As an adult, I have a dominant emotional need to be _____

_____ .

# Your Dominant Emotional Need Is a One-Word Answer to the "Why Questions" of Your Life

Your dominant emotional need is an extremely deep emotional need toward which nearly every action in your adult life is, in some way, focused. This need is what (in your heart of hearts) you desperately want and need from other people in each exchange with them.

Each time someone meets this need in your life, you are temporarily reassured that your phobia is not real. But this reassurance tends to evaporate very quickly, leaving you once again in a needy position.

Seven very clear implications of your dominant emotional need are worthy of note.

## 1. Dominant Emotional Need Is the Focus of Decisions

When you start to make a decision, the real question is, Is this decision going to work toward getting my dominant emotional need met, or will this decision push me more in the direction of my dominant adult phobia?

For example, when we decide to buy a car or house or change jobs, we ask ourselves, Will this decision lead to getting my dominant emotional need (love, significance, admiration, etc.) met? Or will it push me toward my dominant adult phobia (rejection, insignificance, failure, etc.)? We make most of our decisions based on the potential impact on our emotional needs and adult phobias.

## 2. Dominant Emotional Need Is the Basis of Listening

Your emotions are constantly looking for ways to get your dominant emotional need met. You actually reinterpret things someone says to meet your dominant emotional need. A person may make a simple statement: "I like that shirt." That may be the only real meaning in the comment: "I like that shirt; I like the color." But you interpret that as, "The person likes *me.*"

Someone may say, "I like your hair." Maybe the person meant, "I like what the stylist did to your hair." You hear, "The person likes *me.*"

A woman who has a dominant emotional need to be loved may hear the statement: "I like your bracelet." But emotionally, she hears, "The person must like *me* because she likes my bracelet."

### 3. Dominant Emotional Need Is the Basis on Which You Judge Your Relationships

What a person is looking for in a marriage partner is typically someone who does not threaten the dominant adult phobia and appears to be capable of consistently meeting the dominant emotional need. For example, an athlete whose dominant emotional need is to be loved unconditionally may be looking for someone who is not particularly impressed with the Most Valuable Player Awards and the press clippings scrapbook. The athlete is looking for someone who "loves me as a person."

### 4. Dominant Emotional Need Is Often the Basis upon Which You Choose the Groups You Join

When people are attracted to a club, university, or religious group, the song, the message, or the idea that attracted them to the group was probably something that "promised" to meet the dominant emotional need.

For example, the child who feels no love at home, attends vacation Bible school for the first time, and hears the song "Jesus Loves Me" hears a promise of love. Similarly, when an audience listens to a speaker's challenge to "come help change the world," some hear a motivational talk. But the person needing significance hears something different, something almost irresistible. The response is "these are my kind of people. I want to march with these people!"

## 5. Dominant Emotional Need Is the Pivotal Question in a Mid-Life Reevaluation or Crisis

In a mid-life reevaluation one of the most frequently asked questions is, Can the emotionally significant people in my life ever really meet my dominant emotional need? The next question is, Can I live the rest of my life without my dominant emotional need being met? A mid-life crisis happens when the conclusion is "NO"!

Here is where you define your dominant emotional need and become extremely candid with your life mate or soul mate and don't wait for her or him to figure you out. Open up and explain with great clarity, precision, and emotion your dominant emotional need, and seek to understand and meet her or his dominant emotional need as well.

## 6. Dominant Emotional Need Is the Reason You Are Emotionally "Driven"

You will go to outrageous extremes to have the dominant emotional need met. You will push your body, mind, and emotions to the limit at times for one drop of love, respect, significance, and so on. You will work overtime hours and hours and hours to have that need met. You will do whatever it takes to get that need met.

The emptier you feel when your needs go unmet, the more likely you are to self-destruct. As Steve Arter-

71

burn, founder and president of New Life Treatment Centers, says, "The greater our accomplishments that produce little needed satisfaction, the more desperate we become and open to behavior inconsistent with our values."

### 7. Reaching Goals That Don't Meet Your Dominant Emotional Need Is Frequently Experienced as Devastating Disappointment or Disillusionment

You may naively assume if you could reach some "ultimate" goal, it would meet your dominant emotional need once and for all. You assume that you would finally be free of your dominant emotional need and that your dominant adult phobia would be gone forever. When it doesn't happen that way, you're severely disappointed and frankly, many times, disillusioned. At best, meeting the goal results in a temporary meeting of your dominant emotional need.

## Who Do You Hope Will Meet Your Dominant Emotional Need?

Who do you most want to meet your dominant emotional need?

Os Guinness, an internationally known author and speaker, has coined a phrase "an audience of one," which has captured my attention. He says that the truly mature person has "an audience of one, and that One is God!" I agree with Os. This concept remains the ideal.

It has been my experience, however, that being respected or loved by God is not the same as being respected or loved by a fellow human being. Sometimes our emotional needs can best be met through a profound understanding of God, but sometimes it's extremely helpful to have a loving, respectful, accepting human involved in that process.

## Vulnerability Results When a Dominant Emotional Need Goes Unmet

Moral slippage is a major concern.

- *Why* would a minister who knows the difference between right and wrong commit adultery?
- *Why* would a federal judge accept a relatively small bribe and risk being disbarred?
- *Why* would a nation's president take illegal risks that could lead to impeachment?

Just as physical pain is real, so emotional pain is real. This truth could be shown in the following equation:

PHYSICAL PAIN = EMOTIONAL PAIN

Many people who have experienced the loss of a loved one actually say they would much prefer physical pain to emotional pain.

Dr. Joel Robertson is president of the Robertson Neurochemical Institute, Ltd., in Saginaw, Michigan. He specializes in neuropharmacology and the development of self-care systems using brain chemical technology. Dr. Robertson has seen over eleven thousand patients suffering various forms of emotional and physical pain. Listen to his perspective on emotional pain:

> Pain, as we know it, takes many forms, any one of which can be severe in its effect on the healthy functioning of a person. Emotional, physical, and spiritual pain affect a person's perspective of herself or himself, God, and others.
>
> This pain alters intimacy, acceptance, and love that is experienced or given, thereby destroying the healthy components of a relationship. We are relational beings, and our total health is determined by the health of our relationships.
>
> Emotional pain isn't as easily seen as a broken arm or leg, but it hampers a person's wholeness even more. A broken leg or arm will heal without any extra effort by the person, but emotional pain only worsens when ignored.
>
> Eventually emotional pain intensifies to the point that it causes or worsens physical and spiritual decay. High blood pressure, ulcers, arthritis, and allergies are but a few of the illnesses caused by or worsened by emotional pain and stress. Spiritual decay often takes the form of a lack of joy and peace. We are only as happy as the most unhappy part of us.

But a lot of people don't seem to see that emotional need is frequently as powerful in shaping behavior as physical need, sometimes more so. And this truth could be shown in the following equation.

## PHYSICAL NEED = EMOTIONAL NEED

A dominant emotional need is as driving as a physical need. Let me give you an extreme, unrealistic example I often use when speaking to groups to illustrate this vulnerability idea.

Imagine that I make this offer to you: "If you will steal a book for me, I'll give you a glass of fresh water."

However, you just had a drink at the fountain, and you're not thirsty. You say, "Bobb, why do you think I, a moral, upstanding person, would steal a book for you for a glass of water? I'm not even thirsty."

I say, "That's okay, I understand."

But now imagine you've been in the desert for four days under a 119-degree desert sun. Your lips are so dry that they are cracked. You can't swallow anymore, and if you drank any water, you'd have to take it in an eyedropper to keep from messing up your mouth. You're that thirsty. Every cell in your body craves liquid. You're severely dehydrated. You're about to die!

I now come to you with the same proposition: "Look, all you have to do is steal a book. Then I'll give you this large goblet of pure drinking water."

See the difference?

Both equations speak clearly to human behavior.

$$PHYSICAL\ PAIN = EMOTIONAL\ PAIN$$

$$PHYSICAL\ NEED = EMOTIONAL\ NEED$$

Frequently, this level of need leads a person in the opposite direction of all the truth of a lifetime. That's why it becomes such a vulnerable point. For this very reason, senior pastors leave twenty-five-year marriages and pulpits to marry the church secretary, leaving a church full of disillusioned members.

Does that make it right? Of course not! Does that make it ethical or moral or legal? No. Knowing about the power of emotional needs just helps me understand why women run off with men who are not their husbands, and men run off with women who are not their wives.

Many times in an affair the "other" person isn't nearly as attractive (in any obvious way) as the spouse. The person often doesn't have as much money or social standing. Why would someone do that? The "other" person meets a dominant emotional need the spouse has never met, has stopped meeting, cannot meet, or chooses not to meet.

You may say, "Well, I would never do that. I would never steal the book, and I would never have an affair— no matter how needy I became!"

I certainly hope you never get that needy. But be careful saying what you will never do because when you get to a certain point of need (physical or emotional), it really is a major temptation. That's why men and women do things they never dreamed they would do one year earlier.

Your dominant emotional need should be kept confidential to all but trusted close friends because a person can easily take advantage of knowing what you need.

## *Heart of Hearts Reflection*

Not everyone is tempted in the same way. What is very tempting to one person is not tempting at all to the next.

In a reflective moment looking into your heart of hearts, ask yourself, What is my dominant emotional need? Where would I be tempted morally, ethically, or legally to negotiate my values to have my dominant emotional need met?

You need to basically say to yourself, All right, here is where I'm most vulnerable. Anyone who will meet my dominant emotional need consistently has my emotional attention. It's very tempting to me to be attracted to that person or group in an inappropriate way or to do things I normally

77

wouldn't do so they will meet my dominant emotional need. I might be vulnerable to them in some way. So how do I protect myself? Where do I put a self-imposed fence so I don't go any further?

---

The concept of emotionally equal words is very important because husbands and wives have emotional vulnerability points that may be very, very different. Your dominant emotional need may be to be respected. And your spouse's dominant emotional need may be to be loved. The following equation would be *emotionally true*:

RESPECTED = LOVED

Whatever your spouse lists as the dominant emotional need is needed as much, and potentially as desperately, as whatever you list as your dominant emotional need.

A combination I see frequently is a husband who has a deep need for significance and a wife who has a deep need for security. The husband should see, but often does not see, that his wife's need for security is as great as his need for significance. When he comes home talking about a new opportunity to do a job that would be far more significant but would require moving to another city, it .is no wonder that she reacts with resistance. To her it represents a threat to her security.

If the husband were to present the opportunity in terms of "increased salary and therefore more savings and very shortly more financial security," his chances of getting a positive response would be far better.

Frequently it seems impossible to communicate to a person how deeply his or her spouse needs to feel loved, secure, or accepted until the need is presented as something the spouse needs "just as much as you need to be admired" (or appreciated or recognized).

Just as the needs are equal, the dominant adult phobias are equal, whether it's the fear of being rejected socially or the fear of insignificance.

Once you and your spouse understand each other's phobias and needs, it is far easier to be sensitive to your separate vulnerability points. When you are feeling a bit vulnerable, tell your spouse as a major protection against manipulation.

## Vulnerability to Sales Manipulation

We're also vulnerable to manipulation by salespeople in the area of the dominant emotional need. We are potentially vulnerable to seducers, con people, and other kinds of social and relational manipulators.

We are vulnerable, for example, to the automotive company's advertisements that promise we will be noticed if we drive the company's new sports model. The car may actually be inferior to a similar model made by another company as far as price, quality, and mileage, but we buy the car that promises to get us noticed!

In the same way, we are vulnerable to the clothing clerk who promises that a particular dress or suit will be very popular at the party. We believe that we will be recognized or accepted immediately if we just buy this special item.

In general, the salespeople who present their goods or services as leading to being loved, significant, admired, recognized, appreciated, secure, respected, or accepted have our attention.

# A Dominant Emotional Need Is Satisfied Only a Short Time and Then Becomes a Need Again

You have one or more of these dominant emotional needs. These needs can be met for a short period of time. Each time someone meets your needs you are temporarily reassured that your dominant adult phobia is not real.

But because of your dominant childhood feeling and your dominant adult phobia, reassurance seems to evaporate quickly, leaving you once again feeling your dominant emotional need. No matter how many times you receive a compliment intended to meet this dominant emotional need, it's only temporarily reassuring.

When a person says, "I love you," to someone who has been loved unconditionally for a lifetime, the reassurance may last for days. But when a person says, "I love you," to someone who has been loved conditionally for a lifetime, the needy person may soon need to be reassured again. That's because the phobic fear that "this person doesn't really love me and may reject me" crops up again in a matter of minutes or hours.

We humans go to some rather extreme lengths to be reassured that our phobic fears are not real and to make sure that our emotional needs are met regularly. Sometimes when a person expresses admiration for someone who needs to be admired frequently, the needy person will ask for the expression of admiration to be repeated. The person will act as though she or he did not hear clearly, but in reality the person just needs to hear it again!

# Chapter 4

## What Is Your Surest, Safest Style?

*As an adult, you develop what seems to be the surest,*
*safest style (e.g., enabling, leading, or rescuing) of*
*relating to life to guarantee your dominant*
*emotional need will be satisfied.*

You will keep trying new styles until one fulfills the dominant emotional need. You stay with that surest, safest style until it no longer works.

There are eight surest, safest styles adults use in having the dominant emotional need met. Please rate the following items on a scale of 1 to 10:

1 = not emotionally loaded for me

10 = very emotionally loaded for me

Remember, you are free to make any changes you like!

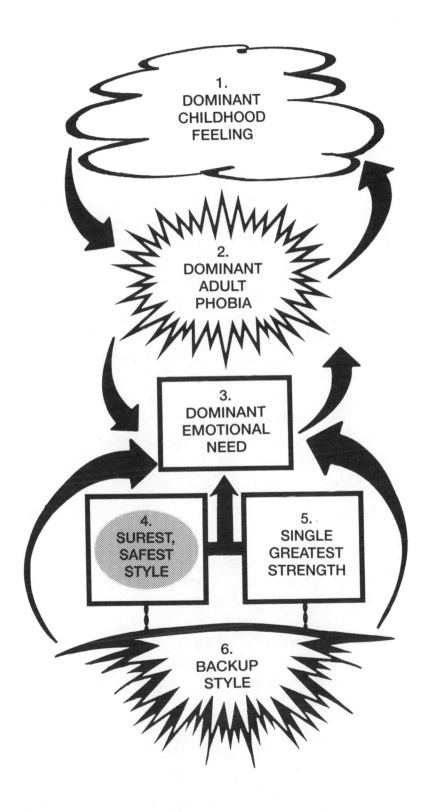

My surest, safest style for having my dominant emotional need met is to play the role of . . .

1. _____ *enabler*.

> That means serving endlessly . . . expecting little in return . . . and making excuses for loved ones who hurt me.

- Earn love by serving those I love
- Enable those I love; help them reach their goals; avoid confronting them with their problems
- Give others what they need
- Make excuses for (cover for) loved ones when they hurt me or others
- Make peace (at nearly all costs); avoid conflict; try to smooth things
- Seek positive progress without seeking credit (glory)
- Other

_____

2. _____ *leader*.

> That means leading people toward a significant goal, cause, or dream.

- Ask profound questions
- Build organizations around dreams
- Dedicate life to a few primary goals and/or dreams

86

- Dream big dreams!
- Make intelligent observations and steady contributions; offer valuable perspective
- Paint crystal clear word pictures of a bright future
- Seek and keep the "big picture"
- Other

3. _____ *promoter.*

 That means making deals . . . taking risks . . . energizing!

- Attack superchallenges requiring great courage
- Catalyze; energize; excite people about projects
- Convince the group "we can do this!"
- Make deals; risk things others would avoid
- Other

4. _____ *entertainer.*

 That means standing out in or from the crowd . . . being noticed!

- Be the life of the party!
- Live with pizazz, style, flair!
- Make a statement; be showy; be sexy; be nontraditional!

87

- Perform; be the center of attention!
- Shock people by doing the unexpected!
- Other

---

5. _____ *rescuer.*

>That means protecting, defending, and helping the underdog or the less fortunate.

- Communicate understanding to the person who currently feels inadequate
- Empower the powerless; help the helpless; love the unloved
- Find a needy person or situation nearly irresistible, frequently neglecting my own responsibilities to help someone who is more needy than I am
- Rescue the needy and threatened
- Other

---

6. _____ *controller.*

>That means getting the situation under control . . . making things secure . . . taking charge.

- Accumulate money; be powerful
- Be very cautious; diversify

- Buy powerful, safe cars, trucks, boats, etc.
- Establish very clear limits, policies, margins, boundaries
- Gather what others consider too much information
- Hire good security as needed
- Other

---

7. _____ *specialist.*

That means being the best at one specific skill. . . knowing the most about one topic. . . or having the most or best of something.

- Be superstrong in one very specific specialty area
- Educate myself; get stronger . . . Stronger . . . STRONGER!
- Rely on the specialty whenever meeting someone who doesn't show proper respect
- Other

---

8. _____ *people pleaser.*

That means being socially popular . . . the person everyone likes.

89

- Bend over backward for others just in case they would not like me if I didn't help them
- Can't say no; overcommitted
- Create an environment where everyone is content
- Help everyone feel accepted and welcome; meet each person's agenda if possible
- Make others happy, even at my expense
- Spend or give too much money to be "in the club"
- Wear fashionable clothes; dress appropriately
- Other

---

Of the eight surest, safest styles, the one I personally use the very most and with the greatest comfort is being a (an)

1. _____ enabler.
2. _____ leader.
3. _____ promoter.
4. _____ entertainer.
5. _____ rescuer.
6. _____ controller.
7. _____ specialist.
8. _____ people pleaser.

The way I would describe my surest, safest style in

my own words would be: As an adult, my surest, safest style of relating to have my dominant emotional need met is by being a (an) _____

_____.

And I also tend to avoid

_____ attention.
_____ commitments.
_____ competing.
_____ confronting.
_____ intimacy.
_____ leadership.
_____ risking.
_____ socializing.

## Heart of Hearts Reflection

If you meet new people and want them to be among the people who meet your dominant emotional need, how do you relate to them? What do you try to be? What do you do? What do you avoid doing?

# The Focus of Your Surest, Safest Style (and Style Changes) Is Typically to Have Your Dominant Emotional Need Met in a Predictable and Consistent Way!

Your emotional assumption is, If only I can be compassionate enough, lead enough, be sexy enough, if only I can accumulate enough money, encourage enough, provide enough, or if only I can avoid competing, confronting, or risking, surely my dominant emotional need can be met *permanently*.

### Special Note to Need Meeters: Enablers, Rescuers, and People Pleasers

To relax, you must get completely away from people. When you're with *any* person, whether a homeless person on the street or a close friend or a family member, your emotional system keeps asking, How can I meet this person's needs? And if I meet the person's needs, surely the person will meet my dominant emotional need.

# The Greater the Threat You Feel That Your Dominant Emotional Need Will Not Be Met, the Smaller Number

# of Style Options Your Emotions Will Let You Consider

Under nonthreatening conditions, you are probably able to relate to life in a wide variety of ways depending on the situation. But under threatening conditions, you revert to your surest, safest style.

When under severe threat, some people react in ways that don't appear to be appropriate or effective. For example, the only thing they can do is

- act.
- counsel.
- enable.
- entertain.
- sell.
- teach.

The less secure you feel, the greater is your need to rely on your surest, safest style, which is the most likely to meet your dominant emotional need.

For example, a school principal whose surest, safest style is controlling may normally act and react in a wide variety of styles (leading, promoting, pleasing people). But under the pressure of having the school board present, he may think only in terms of getting or keeping everyone under control. This is true even though the wisest style in this situation would be that of a leader considering many creative new options.

## Changing Your Surest, Safest Style Typically Requires a Model of the Style You Want to Emulate

We humans do not change our basic style of living easily. Changing without a clear model of what we want to become is extremely difficult. And we are very, very sensitive in the early stages of any behavioral change. If someone makes a comment that embarrasses us, we often stop even trying to change. An illustration may be helpful.

### The Elephant Story

It was eleven o'clock one Friday night. I was sound asleep when the phone rang. On the other end was my friend Duane Pederson, founder of the *Hollywood Free Paper* and now president of Duane Pederson Ministries. He asked, "How would you like to go to Tucson tomorrow?"

"Tucson?" I groaned. "What in the world would we do in Tucson?"

"My friend Bobby Yerkes has a circus playing in Tucson tomorrow, and I would like to go down, get away, clear the cobwebs, and work the circus with him. We'll move some props, have a good time, and be back by ten o'clock tomorrow night."

Now there probably isn't a person alive who hasn't dreamed about running away with the circus as a child. So it didn't take me long to agree to go.

The next morning at seven o'clock our jet lifted off the runway at Los Angeles International Airport headed for Tucson.

When we got there, it was a hot, dusty, windy day at the fairgrounds where the circus was playing. We moved props from one of the three rings to the next, helped in any way we could, and generally got dusty, dirty, tired, and hungry.

During one of the breaks, I started chatting with the man who trains the animals for Hollywood movies. "How is it that you can stake down a ten-ton elephant with the same size stake that you use for this little fellow?" I asked. (The "little fellow" weighed about three hundred pounds.)

"It's easy when you know two things: elephants really do have great memories, but they really aren't very smart. When they are babies, we stake them down. They try to tug away from the stake maybe ten thousand times before they realize that they can't possibly get away. At that point, their 'elephant memory' takes over, and they remember for the rest of their lives that they can't get away from the stake."

We humans are sometimes like elephants. When we are teenagers, someone says, "He's not very handsome, she's not very pretty, they're not very good leaders," and "zap" we drive a mental stake into our minds. Often when we become adults, we are still held back by an inaccurate one-sentence stake put in our minds when we were younger.

Pull up some of the stakes holding you back. Today you are an adult capable of a much wider range of styles than you are using. Let's pull some stakes together!

# Chapter 5

# What Is Your Single Greatest Strength?

*As an adult, you develop a single greatest strength to use with your surest, safest style to meet your dominant emotional need as consistently and as predictably as possible.*

A few years ago I had the privilege of spending four days in a retreat setting in Estes Park, Colorado, with Dr. Peter F. Drucker (the father of modern management) and about twenty-five other presidents, senior pastors, and executive directors.

One of the many extremely valuable ideas from that memorable experience was this bottom line: Find what you do best . . . and do it! Defining the single greatest strength is not a quick or easy task for most people. But I can assure you it is well worth the effort!

There are eight categories of strengths adults develop to have dominant emotional needs met consistently. Please rate the following items on a scale of 1 to 10:

1 = not emotionally loaded for me

10 = very emotionally loaded for me

Remember, you are free to make any changes you like!

In the single greatest strength area, I am at my *very best* when I am . . .

1. _____ *facilitating* a project.
   That includes anticipating what will help a project move smoothly in a positive direction and working to complete the project successfully.

   - Doing what others can't or don't want to do; being the "utility player"; filling in
   - Helping others get the job done
   - Seeing that others get what they want or need
   - Working "behind the scenes"
   - Other

   _____

2. _____ *visualizing* the future.
   That includes anticipating the future . . . seeing new options . . . dreaming new dreams.

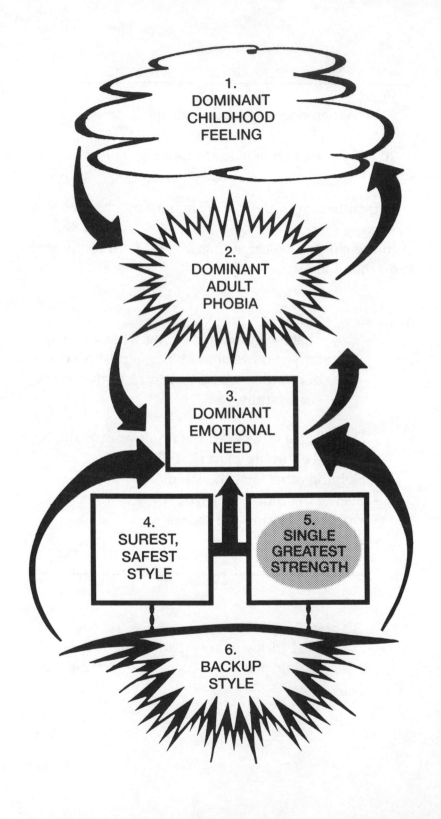

- Asking profound questions
- Framing the "big picture"
- Helping others "see" overlooked potential
- Imagining the future and its implications
- Other

_____

3. _____ *persuading* people to do something.

- Convincing; persuading
- Mobilizing; activating; motivating
- Selling
- Other

_____

4. _____ *entertaining* people.
That includes being center stage and having people watch, take notice, or pay attention.

- Acting; entertaining; doing stand-up comedy
- Being the center of attention
- Competing in anything, from athletic to musical events
- Other

_____

5. _____ *rescuing* the needy.
> That includes noticing injustice and doing something about it and helping those who feel helpless.

- Caring for those who have no one else
- Counseling; listening; empathizing with those who feel inadequate and desperate
- Serving the poorest of the poor
- Other

_____

6. _____ *controlling* a situation.
> That includes retaining or restoring control (financial, physical, social, military, etc.).

- Managing money, people, and/or projects
- Maximizing available resources; improving results
- Working in a clearly structured setting
- Other

_____

7. _____ *specializing*.
> That includes being better at one thing than more than 99 percent of the population.

- Making technical information functional in my area of specialty
- Smashing roadblocks in my specialty area
- Solving what no one else will tackle—"the impossible"—in my specialty
- Other

_____

8. _____ *socializing.*

That includes helping people have a good time in a social setting.

- Accepting, listening, encouraging, noticing, and pleasing socially
- Attending parties and social events
- Being a responsible part of the group
- Unifying any group; being a group peacemaker
- Other

_____

Of the eight categories, my single greatest strength is

1. _____ facilitating.
2. _____ visualizing.
3. _____ persuading.
4. _____ entertaining.
5. _____ rescuing.

6. _____ controlling.
7. _____ specializing.
8. _____ socializing.

The way I would describe my single greatest strength in my own words would be: As an adult, I feel most confident and comfortable when I am _____

_____.

# Each Person Has Both Character Strengths (Who You *Are*) and Achievement Strengths (What You *Do*)

For the past few years one of my favorite questions to ask of a person I like and enjoy being with has been, "What do you see as your single greatest strength?" I was probing to find out what the person felt most comfortable and confident doing.

To my surprise, at first, probably the most frequent response—after a long reflective pause—was something like, "I guess I would say my honesty, faithfulness, compassion, integrity, or loyalty."

I would then explain that there are two kinds of strength: (1) character strength is what we *are* as humans, and (2) achievement strength is what we *do* as humans.

It has become increasingly clear to me that what psychologists call self-concept is simply a comprehensive list of all of the adjectives you'd use to describe yourself positively and/or negatively.

- I am disciplined.
- I am undisciplined.
- I am faithful.
- I am a procrastinator.

The achievement strength is what you *do* best.

- I am best at persuading.
- I am best at entertaining.
- I am best at controlling a situation.
- I am best at socializing.

Your self-concept is a combination of who you *are* and what you *do*.

## "What Do You *Do* the Very Best?" Is One of Life's Most Profound Fog-Cutting Questions!

You start trying to define what you do best in elementary school or junior high and on through senior high. And you keep working until you find it.

Your single greatest strength gives you a unique market or ministry position. A part of what you want to find out is what do you do better than anyone else so you can play that role on the team.

Knowing your single greatest strength is valuable throughout adulthood. But having that knowledge is especially helpful to those in a mid-life reevaluation. I work a lot with executives in mid-life (emotionally foggy) reevaluation who are asking questions like these:

Do I really have any strength?

Where do I really fit?

What do I want to do with the rest of my life?

Focus your energy on using your single greatest strength. Focus at least 85 percent of your time on maximizing your strength, maybe 10 percent on developing your substrength areas, and then 5 percent on correcting the weak areas.

If you are great at visualizing, for instance, you look at the future far more than most people. You see options others do not see. You dream dreams they do not dream. Use this strength any time you can. If you are a restaurant owner, you might use your ability to visualize to anticipate market trends, imagine new ways of feeding people, and dream of restaurants no one else has considered.

# How Can You Identify Your Single Greatest Strength?

As I talk with executives about their single greatest strength, many ask, "Where would I even start?"

The most effective way I have ever found to identify a person's single greatest strength is to begin by asking a series of assessment questions:

What is my uniqueness?

What do I find easy that other people find hard or impossible?

What is exhilarating to me that to most people is threatening or frightening?

What seems so easy to me that I think, *Well, everyone could do this*, but when I look around, no one is?

What do I do best?

What is the strength I build around?

What is the strength I most frequently combine with my surest, safest style to get my dominant emotional need met?

Make a list of all of the things you do very well, and then circle your top ten strengths. Star the top five that seem the most likely candidates to be your single greatest strength. Now identify the top three and then number one. When you can finally say, "My single greatest strength is my ability to ———————————," you have found one of the corner pieces of your life's ten-thousand-piece puzzle.

## *Heart of Hearts Reflection*

Very honestly speaking, there are likely many areas where you are far above average. There may be many areas where you are stronger than your friends. But the bottom line question for you to wrestle with in the privacy of your heart is: What do I *do* the very best?

Frequently, people can come up with a cluster of three, and they say, "My single greatest strength is one of these three, but I can't quite figure out which one I really do best." In that case, it may take a week or a month to come to a crystal clear perspective. You may want to ask a friend which of the three you do best. Or the friend may have seen you do something else exceptionally well that you have overlooked.

Your strength may be summarized by an unusual word such as *conceptualist* or *piercer*. You feel this word best describes your single greatest strength regardless if anyone else has used this particular term as you are using it. If you could put into one common or uncommon word what you do the very best, what would it be? _____

## All of Your Life Experiences Can Be Used to Build Your Single Greatest Strength

Your dominant childhood feeling results in a dominant adult phobia, which creates a dominant emotional need that is never fully satisfied. So you take each of life's experiences and use it to build your single greatest strength.

See your childhood with adult eyes as having built into you the single greatest strength you have today, and be thankful for the strength rather than resentful of the childhood hurts. *This one thought often allows a person to exchange resentment for thankfulness.*

For example, your childhood may have been insecure, unsafe, unstable, and vulnerable. But today you are a great financial controller for your company. Part of your ability to control comes from that insecure childhood. So be thankful, not for your insecure childhood, but for the strength in controlling it resulted in.

109

# Chapter 6

---

# What Is Your
# Backup Style?

*You have a backup style to use just in case the combination of surest, safest style and single greatest strength fails to get your dominant emotional need met.*

Each person has a not-so-positive way of getting the dominant emotional need met in case the surest, safest style and the single greatest strength combination fails. It is the backup style that, under pressure, will occasionally cross moral, ethical, and potentially even legal lines to have the dominant emotional need satisfied.

Every person on earth has this "dark side," even though we don't see some people's backup style as quickly as others.

The backup style frequently combines a strength with force or power or pressure. In other words, it takes something that's naturally good and puts so much force, power, or pressure with it that it becomes a manipulative, demanding, negative backup style.

Frequently, we are reluctant to admit, accept, and deal with the very fact that we have a backup style. To those of us who are perfectionistic, admitting we have a backup style means admitting we are less than perfect. And less than perfect emotionally means, "I'm *not perfect*. Therefore, I'm *not worthy* of love. So admitting that I'm not perfect is a major step."

But for most people, it's just saying, "Now, realistically, here's how I do it." And like the apostle Paul said, "What I don't want to do I do, and what I want to do I don't."

Recently, Dr. Joel Robertson asked me to give him my thoughts on compulsive behavior, and so I wrote the following free verse.

### Why?

Why?
Why?
Why . . . do I do what I do?

Why . . . do I not do
what I do not do?

Why . . . do . . . I . . . keep . . . on . . . doing . . .
what I don't want to do?

Why . . . do I stop doing
what I have so firmly resolved to do
on goal-setting days?

113

Why . . . as an adult
      do I find it
      so hard
      to admit my needs
         and the
         insecurity
         of my childhood?

Why . . . is it surprising to me
      when the crack of brain light
      called
      insight
      lets me see the connection
      between
            past . . . present . . . future?

Why . . . is it so difficult to let the world
      see the me that my friends see
      or
      my friends see the me I see?

Why?

There are eight backup styles adults use frequently. Please rate the following items on a scale of 1 to 10.

1 = not emotionally loaded for me

10 = very emotionally loaded for me

Remember, you are free to make any changes you like!

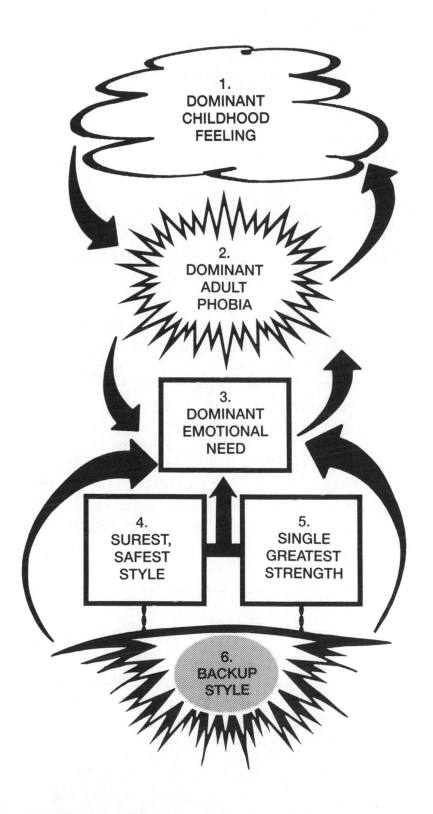

When I get threatened, I am embarrassed to admit it, but I occasionally resort to . . . (Remember, at this point, you are admitting this only to yourself. Be boldly honest with yourself!)

1. _____ *perfectionism.*
> That includes trying to *perform* perfectly to feel *worthy* of *love*.

- Becoming very concerned or depressed with my own failure; refusing to be forgiving with myself
- Doing far more than required (110 percent when 80 percent is needed or wanted)
- Eliminating as much "gray" as possible; staying with "black and white" answers
- Seeing people and situations as all good or all bad
- Trying even harder to do it "right"
- Using excessive guilt to control people
- Other

---

2. _____ *manipulating* people mentally.
> That includes intimidating emotionally or intellectually and outsmarting people.

- Appearing to have health problems, hypochondria
- Giving an intimidating "hard look"
- Making "subtle" hurtful comments
- Playing "mind games" to control people
- Relying on manipulative silence, pouting, attention-getting "depressions"
- Other

---

3. _____ *cutting corners.*

   That includes going around systems, structures, and rules to get where I want to go!

- Cheating the IRS, the company, and/or friends
- Competing with peers for the team leader's attention
- Finding shortcuts to success; ignoring rules
- Lying—expanding, hiding, or shading the truth
- Stealing ideas, perks, or money
- Other

---

4. _____ *extreme behavior.*

   That includes demanding attention by actions or appearance!

117

- Becoming a party "show-off," the "clown"
- Dressing in flashy, showy clothing and even in
bizarre clothing if required to get attention
- Getting "in your face"; intimidating emotionally
and/or verbally.
- Other

_____

5. _____ *workaholism.*
That includes working harder and for
longer hours . . . emotionally hiding in or
at work where it is emotionally safer.

- Becoming a "robot" with a checklist
- Sacrificing the rest of life for my work
- Working harder; digging deeper; being stronger
- Other

_____

6. _____ *overcontrolling.*
That includes insisting people follow the
rules . . . becoming rigid and demanding . . . forcing people.

- Arguing until I get my own way; standing my
ground!

- Being physically aggressive and/or intimidating; bullying; fighting!
- Competing to win at "all costs"
- Having a fiercely independent attitude—I can make it!
- Overeating; when my world is out of control, I control the food I eat; when I feel insecure, eating feels secure
- Overnegotiating
- Taking over!
- Using physical intimidation or force if required to get people "in line"
- Other

---

7. _____ *withdrawing from or avoiding situations* where I feel intimidated.

- Accepting second place when I want first
- Cranking up the stereo and ignoring reality for a while
- Escaping into "depression dropout"
- Escaping into substance abuse
- Escaping to sports
- Quitting; dropping out altogether
- Settling for less; reducing life-style

- Withdrawing; retreating; distancing self
- Other

_____

8. _____ *withdrawing from people* before they can reject me.

- Breaking off relationships; brushing people off
- Decreasing a person's importance in my mind
- Going to another group; never looking back
- Polarizing the group—"us against them"
- Shutting people out with thick, high walls
- Other

_____

Of the eight most common adult backup styles, I most commonly resort to

1. _____ perfectionism.
2. _____ manipulating people mentally.
3. _____ cutting corners.
4. _____ extreme behavior.
5. _____ workaholism.
6. _____ overcontrolling.
7. _____ withdrawing from situations.
8. _____ withdrawing from people.

The way I would describe my backup style in my own words would be: As an adult, the backup style to which I resort under pressure is to

_____.

## Note

It is perfectly okay to go back over chapters 1 through 6 and change any of your answers as you see more clearly what was actually emotionally significant in your childhood. Frequently, what at first seemed to rate an emotionally loaded 10 turns out to be a 3 or 4. And what at first seemed to rate a 2 becomes a 10+! Change as much and as often as you like.

# The Vast Majority of Negative Behavior Is Actually a Backup Style

Whenever you see someone doing any type of negative behavior, the person's dominant emotional need is probably not being met.

Some people don't have what they consider a sure, safe style or a single greatest strength, so they start every relationship using their backup style.

A friend who spent time in prison told me of a large inmate who came up to him the day my friend arrived. The inmate's first words were not "Hi, my name is Joe. Can I help you get settled in any way?" (leader and visualizer). They were "Hey, you're wearing my shirt. Give me my shirt!" (manipulator and intimidator).

121

The inmate demanding the shirt had no confidence in his leadership or visualizing skills, so he started the conversation with his backup style.

Then there is the mother who told me her fifteen-year-old daughter sports a fifteen-inch bright blue Mohawk hairstyle. The teenager desperately wants to be recognized. But instead of attempting to be noticed in more conventional ways, she started with extreme behavior. She demanded the attention of everyone, even first-time acquaintances.

Understanding the use of backup styles certainly doesn't excuse negative behavior, but it does explain most of it. Without a clear single greatest strength and without a clear surest, safest style, a person is left to rely almost entirely on backup style, which typically destroys relationships, and leads to the use of the backup style even faster in the next threatening situation.

## A Single Greatest Strength Used to Extreme Often Becomes Negative and Counterproductive

### Perfectionism

Many of us have grown up in homes or schools built on conditional love, acceptance, or praise. What happens all too frequently is that a parent or a teacher communicates to a child, in essence, "If you perform at a higher level, I will give you more love." The child, being a "love sponge," becomes performance driven.

122

The word *performance* to a perfectionist is one of those extraordinarily emotionally loaded words, just like *worthy*.

A small child concludes, "If I can never please my parents, I don't feel worthy of being loved. Therefore, if I'm not perfect, I'm not worthy of love at all!"

A perfectionist also frequently experiences in the emotional system a feeling that things are all good or all bad. The perfectionist finds it *almost impossible to admit failure* because, "If I fail, I'm a total failure. I'm all good or all bad, all right or all wrong. There is no in between."

Being unable to admit failure and being driven to be accepted set up a perfectionistic pattern. It isn't just that you want quality workmanship or have high standards.

The difference between having high standards and being a perfectionist is that the perfectionist feels, "If I don't do it perfectly, I'm not worthy of love." A person with high standards says, "I like to do it well so I'll get praise and recognition and appreciation, but if I don't, if it isn't perfect, I'm still worthy of being loved just because I'm me."

The perfectionist is driven to perfection even when it is not required. Perfectionism has become a backup style.

## Work

Many people list working hard as a surest, safest style. But workaholism is a counterproductive hiding at work from other areas of life. Workaholics have a higher percentage of their dominant emotional needs met at work than they do at home or any other place. That's why they stay at work so much.

Workaholics typically feel less awkward on the job. A lot of people feel awkward in life. They don't know what to say; they don't know how to say it; they don't quite know what to do or how to do it. But at work there is a very precise pattern and they can fit into that, and coworkers meet the dominant emotional need for respect, appreciation, etc.

# Typically, We Will Use Our Backup Style Faster and Will Go to More Dangerous Extremes to Keep Our Needs Being Met Than We Will to Have Our Needs Met Initially

News reports frequently tell of a jealous husband who has killed his wife's lover. The wife has met the husband's need for love for several years. But when he finds out about the lover, the husband fears his wife will stop meeting his need for love.

In most cases, the husband would never have considered killing the other men his wife was dating before he married her. She wasn't meeting his need for love (or intimacy) yet, so there was no threat. But after they were married and she was meeting his need for love, he would actually kill to continue having his need met.

Or consider the example of a person who would never lie to get a position but once in the position would lie to keep it.

Imagine that your dominant emotional need is being completely or at least regularly satisfied, and then someone comes along who threatens to destroy whatever or whoever is meeting your dominant emotional need. What would be your instinctive response?

Human beings will go to more dangerous extremes to make sure needs keep being met than to get the dominant emotional need met initially.

## Every Person Turns to the Backup Style When Threatened

Some people are fragile enough that threat is everywhere. Most people know someone who is really an emotionally underdeveloped three-year-old in the personal self. This person may have a public image that gives the impression of having it "all together." But the person knows that inside he is like a little child.

Such people are extremely fragile. They are difficult to relate to because you get hard, brittle responses from them. They are inflexible.

The stronger the surest, safest style and the single greatest strength, the less need for using the backup style.

Consider the person who has a well-developed style of relating to needy people and whose strength is rescuing those who have been done an injustice. Typically that person's need for appreciation is met without the person's resorting to workaholism.

---

## *This person is like a twenty-foot ceramic shell one-sixty-fourth-inch thick.*

---

A friend I'll call Tom felt inadequate as a child and is a rescuer of people as an adult. He is the director of a rescue mission and receives many words of appreciation from the people he helps. Tom has little need to be a workaholic. However, when he gets no appreciation at home, he stays late at work and begins to move toward workaholism.

We all understand that we have self-protective backup style behavior if someone were threatening to kill us. We also have backup styles when we feel threatened emotionally. What threatens us emotionally is the feeling that someone is going to do something that causes the dominant emotional need to go unmet or stop being met.

When we're being threatened, the thought of processing anything, sleeping twenty-four hours on it, or calling a friend goes right out the window. The intensity is so great to have the need met or the threat stopped that we act instinctively.

That's why it's a good idea to stay away as much as possible from the extreme need of being in the desert for four days without water, so to speak. As strange as it seems, we'll steal a book as fast to survive *emotionally* as we will to survive *physically*. That's backup style.

### Even a Servant Has a Backup Style

Serving is frequently a person's surest, safest style. But being taken for granted results in a backup style

*Bottom line:
If a person freely gives you the surest, safest style but you do not meet that person's dominant emotional need, expect the backup style sooner or later.*

response because of the need to have the dominant emotional need met. It's a pattern I've seen over and over again.

A child who needs to be recognized will disrupt a classroom a little bit, always raising his hand, talking too much, making little noises, or answering without permission. If you simply ignore him and tell the class to just ignore him, you can count on seeing progressively extreme behavior.

## When a Spouse or Close Friend Uses a Backup Style, Search for Creative New Ways to Meet the Dominant Emotional Need to Reduce the Threat Being Felt

The backup style combination of spouses or close friends is critical in determining how they will resolve conflict. If one is always aggressive and the other always withdraws, guess what happens when arguments start?

If the behavior is extreme, try recognizing and paying attention to your mate, and the extreme behavior will lessen. For example, if your mate is a perfectionist and on a particular day seems to be going to an extreme, tell your mate how much you truly love him or her.

According to Steve Arterburn,

Marriage Counseling is often a process of getting two people to stop using their backup style and start using their strengths. It also focuses each mate on the other's needs. When those needs are met, the need to use the backup style is reduced.

## *Heart of Hearts Reflection*

How do you act or react when your dominant emotional need is not being met or there is a threat that your dominant emotional need will no longer be met?

In a totally honest moment with yourself, ask, How would I describe my backup style?

# Chapter 7

## Fitting the Puzzle Pieces Together

Working out the following ten steps will take some time. Relax and enjoy the process of putting together the puzzle.

You can't really do it wrong. Just keep working on it, and sooner or later it will be done and be clear!

Remember, you are trying to identify the emotionally loaded pieces of your life. In short, you're trying to summarize your "why pattern."

1. *Fill in the "Why People Do What They Do" chart with numbers from the appropriate pages.*

Use a pencil. It's okay to change your mind.

- Column A—"Dominant Childhood Feeling"— see pages 23–29.
- Column B—"Dominant Adult Phobia"—see pages 46–52.
- Column C—"Dominant Emotional Need"—see pages 62–68.
- Column D—"Surest, Safest Style"—see pages 84–91.
- Column E—"Single Greatest Strength"—see pages 98–104.
- Column F—"Backup Style"—see pages 114–121.

2. *Add up the numbers across each of the eight bands to get a total number of points per band.*

The higher the total number, the more important that band is in your "why pattern."

**45–60 points: Extremely Important**

This band in your emotional-motivational pattern affects nearly all of your adult behavior in some way. It is a major source of drive or drivenness.

**30–44 points: Important**

This band in your "why pattern" affects much of your adult behavior but is not likely your major source of drive.

**0–29 points: Relatively Unimportant**

Unless there is a box numbered 8, 9, or 10 somewhere in this band, you can basically ignore it for now. The band occasionally affects your behavior but typically *not* in a major way.

# Why You Do What You Do

| | A DOMINANT CHILDHOOD FEELINGS | B DOMINANT ADULT PHOBIA | C DOMINANT EMOTIONAL NEED |
|---|---|---|---|
| 1 | CONDITIONALLY LOVED OR UNLOVED ☐ | REJECTION (PERSONAL) ☐ | LOVED UNCONDITIONALLY ☐ |
| 2 | DESTINED, BLESSED, SPECIAL ☐ | INSIGNIFICANCE ☐ | SIGNIFICANT (MAKE A DIFFERENCE) ☐ |
| 3 | FAVORED (BY ADULTS OVER PEERS) ☐ | FAILURE (LOSS OF FAVORED POSITION) ☐ | ADMIRED (AS GROUP "HERO") ☐ |
| 4 | IGNORED (EMOTIONALLY) ☐ | INVISIBILITY ☐ | RECOGNIZED ☐ |
| 5 | INADEQUATE (TO MEET EXPECTATIONS) ☐ | FAILURE (INADEQUATE PERFORMANCE) ☐ | APPRECIATED ☐ |
| 6 | INSECURE ☐ | DEPENDENCE, ABANDONED ☐ | SECURE ☐ |
| 7 | INTIMIDATED (BY ANOTHER PERSON) ☐ | FAILURE (TO BECOME AN ADULT) ☐ | RESPECTED ☐ |
| 8 | UNACCEPTABLE (SOCIALLY) ☐ | REJECTION (SOCIAL) ☐ | ACCEPTED FOR WHO I REALLY AM ☐ |

| D | E | F |
|---|---|---|
| **SUREST, SAFEST STYLE** | **SINGLE GREATEST STRENGTH** | **BACKUP STYLE** |
| ENABLER ☐ | FACILITATING ☐ | ☐ PERFECTIONISM |
| LEADER ☐ | VISUALIZING ☐ | MANIPULATING PEOPLE MENTALLY ☐ |
| PROMOTER ☐ | PERSUADING, SELLING ☐ | CUTTING CORNERS ☐ |
| ENTERTAINER ☐ | ENTERTAINING ☐ | EXTREME BEHAVIOR ☐ |
| RESCUER (NEEDED BY NEEDY) ☐ | RESCUING ☐ | WORKAHOLISM (HIDING AT WORK) ☐ |
| CONTROLLER ☐ | CONTROLLING ☐ | OVERCONTROLLING, INTIMIDATING ☐ |
| SPECIALIST ☐ | SPECIALIZING ☐ | WITHDRAWING FROM SITUATIONS ☐ |
| PEOPLE PLEASER ☐ | SOCIALIZING ☐ | WITHDRAWING FROM PEOPLE (BEFORE THEY REJECT ME) ☐ |

## Notes

This rating system is not an absolutely scientific method. Using the rating system gives you an objective way to communicate or weigh your subjective feelings. In essence, it is a way for you to "take your own pulse," for you to see how strongly you feel about certain words or phrases.

You can easily fool this system. But it is my assumption that your focus is deep self-understanding. Be honest with yourself.

3. *Identify the top three bands (the top three highest numbers).*

What is the number one band? This one probably influences your adult behavior the *very most* today.

Does the number one band "by the numbers" feel like the most powerful to you emotionally as you reflect on it? It should. If it doesn't, which band does? It is okay to change!

If you have two bands that have about the same number of total points, think about both bands over a period of a week. Score each box again and see if one now has a higher number of points. If the two bands are still about the same, simply relax and assume that you have two major needs and at different points in your life you will have two fears, two needs, two styles, two strengths, and two backup styles.

4. *Identify your three most emotionally loaded boxes (there are forty-eight boxes—eight down and six across) anywhere on the chart.*

Circle the box on the chart that feels the very most important to you. This box is vital in understanding why you do what you do.

5. *Look at any boxes with low scores (under 5) in your top three bands.*

Each box in your number one band should be fairly high. You may want to rethink any low score box and rescore it if it now seems higher than you had originally felt. If no score change is needed, leave it like it is.

6. *Look at isolated high scoring boxes (8 or higher) that are not in one of your top three bands.*

Any single high scoring box could uncover a major new band, or it could be just an isolated box. Consider the possibilities. Each band is a pattern that explains why you do what you do. Band number 1 explains the perfectionist pattern, band number 5 explains the workaholic pattern, and so forth.

You should now feel very confident in your top one to three "why patterns." There should be very little question in your mind about the logical relationships of your "why pattern." If you have a question, you may want to let it set for a day or two and return to your reflections with a fresh mind.

You now know logically *why you do what you do!*

137

7. *Fill out the following summary.*

The following is a logical look at how my "why pattern" works.

As a child, the dominant childhood feeling I felt was

_____.

(See page 29.)

As a result, I have a dominant adult phobia of

_____.

(See page 52.)

To assure me that my phobia is not real, I have a dominant emotional need to be

_____.*

(See page 68.)

To have my emotional need met, the surest, safest style I know of relating to life is as a (an)

_____.

(See page 91.)

---

*An extremely high percentage of why I do what I do is to make sure my dominant emotional need is met. And when this need is not met, I become progressively vulnerable to anyone who offers to meet this need.

I have also worked to develop a single greatest strength. I am at my very best when I am

_____.

(See page 104.)

I combine my surest, safest style and my single greatest strength as the *most* predictable, dependable way to have my dominant emotional need met as consistently as possible. When this combination fails to get my dominant emotional need met, I also have developed a backup style where I resort to

_____.

(See page 121.)

8. *Remember the basic logic of the "why pattern."*

As an adult, you typically

use your single greatest strength

combined with your surest, safest style

to guarantee that your dominant emotional need will be met,

temporarily reassuring you that your dominant adult phobia is not real

and that your dominant childhood feelings are under control.

139

> If the above fails, you move to your
> backup style and try to force the is-
> sue!

9. *Take some time to think about your emotional mysteries.*

You should now see why you have done or not done many things in the past. Mysteries solved!

To identify your "why pattern" using the "Why People Do What They Do" chart, the easiest boxes to start with will likely be your dominant childhood feeling, your dominant adult phobia, and your dominant emotional need.

However, working with the chart to find what friends and family members need from you is different. The fastest way to determine another person's "why pattern" is to identify the surest, safest style, the single greatest strength, and the backup style. Once these three are clear, it is easy to imagine the person's dominant emotional need that you should try to meet.

10. *Read chapter 8 with your "why pattern" in mind.*

Begin to experience healing for some of the hurts in your history.

Chapter 8

---

# Healing the Hurts
# from History

Typically, understanding how your emotional system
works and how the pieces of your emotional puzzle fit

*Start with whichever
section sounds the
most appealing to
you. There is no
implied order to this
list of ten, except the
very first one.*

together makes a great deal of difference in the ability to resolve the past and capitalize on your strengths. Here are ten very specific ways to heal your historic hurts.

# 1. Start with Your Parents

Parents are by far the most common source of emotional pain I have seen in the past twenty years. If you need to heal a few hurts with your parents some specific steps have proven extremely practical and helpful for my clients and for me personally.

### Practical Steps to Healing the Hurts of Childhood with Your Parents

**As you are thinking about your parents, call them by their first names,** *not Mom and Dad. You can see them more adult-to-adults than emotionally needy child to perfect parents. You get a more adult view of your childhood.*

Caution: Do not start calling your mother and father by their first names when you are with them. I'm not talking about that. But when you're thinking to yourself, trying to resolve your relationship, this simple technique adjusts the expectations for the "ideal mother" and "ideal father" learned from greeting cards and from Mother's Day and Father's Day celebrations. Remember, parents were only imperfect people trying to do the best they knew how, which in some cases was not always that great.

Mentally calling your parents by their first names often takes some of the emotional sting out of negative childhood memories. As you understand your parents more as flesh-and-blood imperfect human beings, you may see your childhood in a very different light.

*Study your grandparents.* Upon careful examination, you may determine that your parents were "victims" of your grandparents' homes. They have done the best job they could of raising you, but because of their upbringing, they may have actually been children raising a child and couldn't have been expected to do it perfectly the first time through.

Therefore, you may find it profitable to study your grandparents. Study the relationship between your mother and your father and your grandparents. Talk with your grandparents, your parents, and your aunts and uncles about your childhood.

Ask your father's brothers and sisters, if possible, to talk to you about your dad growing up, what he was like, what they saw, what they experienced, what their relationship was with him. And do the same with your mother's side of the family.

Understanding your parents in this way will give you a whole different perspective.

*Establish your parents' emotional age in your mind.* Ask yourself, in terms of healing the past, How old is Mom or Dad emotionally? At what age did one or both have a trauma? Did you possibly outgrow your mother or your father at age six or seven?

*If* your parents had a traumatic cap put on their lives at age four, five, or six, it's possible that by the time you were in junior high school, you were older than your parents emotionally. They were trying to parent you when in reality they may have been "emotional children." (If you think your parents may have been emotional children, see the story in Appendix 1:2. "Dangerous Assumption 2.")

If your parents are still emotional children because of a trauma in their early years, this insight may well resolve much of the pain in your past almost instantly.

Assume you are stronger than your parents emotionally. Whenever we meet a person we go through a split-second evaluation of who is emotionally stronger at that particular instant in time. We do this with our mates, our dates, our friends, with strangers, and with our parents.

For example, let's assume for a minute that your child came home from school and said, "Can we talk for a minute?" You may respond, "Not now. I've had a bad day, and I'm right in the middle of a phone conversation." You have just assessed that your needs are greater at the moment than the child's needs.

But let's change the scene. Let's assume that you are in the same situational pressure when your son comes in the door sobbing. His friends have just called him ten bad names and kicked him out of the club. You sense that his needs at the moment are greater than your own. You excuse yourself and hang up the phone.

Parents and children have sensors that tell each other who has the greatest needs at the moment.

If we sense others are stronger, we rely on their

strength. If we sense we're stronger, we let them rely on our strength.

Now, think about your parents for a minute. Most typically, a child goes home assuming that parents are emotionally stronger. Adult children frequently go "home" as needy children, hoping their parents will meet needs for love, appreciation, and/or security. They rarely realize that at this very moment their parents may need the child's reassurances even more.

*Take the initiative with your parents emotionally.* One danger of understanding your personal "why pattern" is waiting passively for other people (like your parents) to meet your dominant emotional need now that you are precisely aware of it.

*May I suggest that you make a game out of meeting your parents' needs? Look for signals of what they need from you, and take the initiative.*

Turn to the "Why You Do What You Do" chart in chapter 7, and look under the "Surest, Safest Style" column. Based on observable style, what would you say is each parent's dominant emotional need? Try meeting these needs in your parents for a while and see how they respond.

Caution: You may think you've completely resolved your less-than-ideal relationship with your parents by understanding their "why patterns" logically. But when you actually see your parents, all of those old negative emotions may instantly pop back with one word, one phrase, or one glance. Don't be discouraged. Relax and just *keep making progress!*

## *Heart of Hearts Reflection*

Can you imagine the difference it would make in your relationship with your parents if you were to actually carry out these suggestions? You may also want to make a list and thank them for anything and everything they did, or even tried to do, right in your childhood!

## 2. Keep a Positive Focus About Your Past

Every childhood had its share of "hard knocks." Some had far more than their share. The point is, you may find it helpful to focus on the good parts of your childhood—whatever the good parts may be and no matter how small they may be.

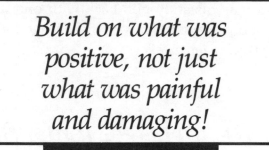

*Build on what was positive, not just what was painful and damaging!*

If it isn't too far a stretch, try to see that even the parent you feel the least resolved with, the most bitterness toward, the most concern for, or the most frustration with probably did or tried to do something right when you were a child.

Make a list of the things your parents did right, the strengths they had, and what they tried to do right. What they did right may be as simple as preparing your meals, buying the food, doing your laundry, making your bed, or making you go to school. Keep these positives in mind as a balance to the hurts you feel still need to be healed.

Keeping a positive perspective may not heal the past, but at least it gives additional perspective that allows healing to begin to take place.

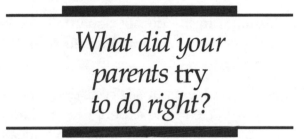

# *What did your parents try to do right?*

Dennis Batterbee, Ph.D., and Gayla Batterbee, Ph.D., are a husband-and-wife team who help "at risk" teenagers. They work very successfully in keeping troubled teens in high school. They teach teenagers the following principles about the process of healing and keeping a positive focus on the future:

1. Regardless of the situation, we are in control of our future; we are not helpless victims.

2. It is important to stay focused on the visual picture of where you would like to be in life and what you would like to become.

3. Taking responsibility for one's actions and

learning from past mistakes are essential to taking charge of one's life.

4. Do not depend on others for your happiness. True peace comes from God and the abilities that He has given us to overcome any situation.

5. Mistakes in life do not equal failure. What is significant is what is learned from these experiences.

6. When problems arise, consider them a challenge, a learning experience, and an opportunity for new and innovative ideas to be utilized.

7. The word *can't* is not in the dictionary, which leaves us with the challenge that all things are possible.

8. One key to success is realizing that there is always room for growth.

9. Enjoyment for today may need to be sacrificed to allow for a better tomorrow.

10. Depression can often be traced back to a lack of action, which means backing away from something that needs to be said or done.

Even though these principles are typically used with troubled teenagers, they are great reminders for us as adults as well to keep positive in our outlook toward the future!

# 3. Reframe Your History

Consider replacing thoughts like this one coming from a child's heart—*Dad worked all of the time . . . ignored me . . . didn't love me*—with an adult reframing—*Actually Dad loved me. He was just a stoic who couldn't say, "I love you," except by providing, just as his father and grandfather before him did. Oh, he really loved me, even though he could never bring himself to utter the actual words, "I love you!"*

If I had asked your father, "How do you tell your children you love them?" he may have said, "I provide for them." And if I then had asked, "Do you mean every time you provided something you were trying to say, 'I love you'?" he may have said, "Of course. How else would I say it? I'm a stoic."

He may have really loved you, though he may have never said, "I love you." That's reframing the past. It isn't changing it; it is simply seeing it more through adult eyes.

Reframing some of your childhood memories can heal the emotional child who felt ignored and unloved but in reality was loved very deeply by a stoic parent or parents.

Sometimes we need to put words into parents' mouths and then confirm our assumptions: "Is that how you feel, Dad?" This technique is still reframing.

I've told many executives, "Look, your dad did not

151

have the ability to say what you wanted him to say in the past and still doesn't. But he would probably like to tell you how he feels. So, what I'd like to encourage you to do is write out how you think or hope he feels, take it to him, and have him read it. Say, 'Dad, I think this is the way you felt about me. Is it?'"

For example, someone could say, "I think you thought that by providing, you were saying, 'I love you,' and I think you may have even thought you told me you loved me occasionally. I don't remember, but I think you probably did. So, I'm assuming that occasionally you actually told me you loved me, even if I don't remember it. And that by providing, you were saying that you loved me, cared for me, and wanted to see me do well in life."

Or someone could say, "It's my guess that when you were watching me play baseball, even though you saw that I didn't do it perfectly and that I could improve, you were proud of me when I'd get a hit or make an out. Even though you sat in the stands and never clapped and never cheered, I assumed that in your heart you were proud of me or you wouldn't have come to the game."

Just write it all out and hand it to your dad or mother; have him or her read it and correct what wasn't right. He or she may say, "That's 100 percent right. That's exactly how I saw it. I'm glad you put it into words. I wouldn't have put it into words, but that's how I felt." His or her saying, "I wouldn't have put it into words,"

152

basically lets you reframe all of your childhood memories in a far more positive light.

### Scriptural Reframing

Another way of reframing hurts of the past is being thankful for them. Scripture says, "In everything give thanks." We are to give thanks even for the worst things that happened to us partly because they helped develop our adult strengths.

That's reframing.

Children misread adults. Adults may unconditionally love children, but if they don't say so, the children may not believe or experience it emotionally.

Reframing goes back and looks with adult eyes at what happened as a child and puts it in a new frame and tests it with the adult involved. Frequently, healing comes from this reframing.

## 4. Discuss Your Past with Your Siblings

Siblings often add a fresh, sometimes far more objective, perspective to childhood memories. Remember that a child's perception of a house may be very different from the house actually lived in as a youngster. Just so, your perceptions of certain emotions may not have been accurate.

Occasionally, asking an older brother or sister, "What really happened when I _____?" brings a very different perspective to your childhood hurts. Many times just seeing things through a brother's or sister's eyes instantly heals the emotional pain in a long-term memory.

Once you are comfortable with sharing your "why pattern," have thought it through, and are really clear on what it is and why it works, you may want to sit down with your brother or sister and explain your "why pattern."

Conversations at this point can go something like this:

SIBLING: "I never meant to make you feel bad just because you were my younger sister (or brother). I was always proud of you."

YOU: "You were? You always told me what I was doing wrong."

SIBLING: "Well, that was just to help you do better. I was proud of you."

Just like conversation heals relationships with parents, sometimes conversations with siblings in a nonaccusatory but clarifying way—which lets them see how you looked at it, how you felt, and what it meant to you—can be healing.

# 5. Seek Fresh Perspective

Ask a mentor or a close friend to hear you out and give you perspective. Sometimes having a mentor, someone who cares for you, respects you, accepts you, and loves you, take an hour or two, or day or two, to let you talk through some of your "why pattern" brings healing.

Frequently, the person's wisdom brings a new perspective that someone within the family can't bring because a family member makes the same assumptions you do. But someone outside the family may make very different assumptions that can shed a healing light on the situation.

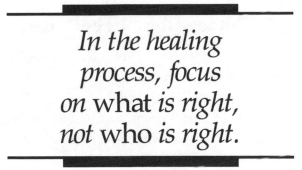

*In the healing process, focus on* what *is right, not* who *is right.*

As you gain more and more trust in your mentor, ask for perspective on the realism of your expectations of childhood. You may find that your expectations were far too high or far too low. Either way, some of your hurt may be healed.

A close friend may not be a wise counselor who can give brilliant new insight into your concerns. But talking about it, saying it, putting it into words, sometimes helps!

I spoke to a small group of executives the other day. A woman came up to me afterward and said, "You know, sometimes when I just talk to a friend, saying it lets me hear how silly it really sounds. Some things I have to hear before I know whether I really believe them or not."

Sometimes the things you are keeping in your heart, the things troubling you, would go away if you'd talk to a friend about them. Talking with a trusted friend can sometimes heal things that don't need to be hurts any longer.

## 6. Review the "I Feel" List

If you have a tendency to deny how you really feel on a given issue or you were raised in a very stoic home, this list can help a lot! (See Appendix 1:10.) Follow the instructions to circle the ones you feel at the moment, double circle the intense ones, star the top ten, double star the top three, and triple star the most dominant one.

How do you really feel in a given situation today as an adult? Asking this question is another way to find healing from past hurts. How did you *actually* feel as a child?

## 7. Pray Through Your "Why Pattern"

You may want to consider going back through this book and praying your way through each section. Ask God for insight, wisdom, and healing.

Praying your way through the "why pattern" as an adult often brings healing perspective because it helps you look at your hurts and your history from an eternal viewpoint.

## 8. Change Your Audience

In looking at why you do what you do, I've concluded that unless you change your audience you will rarely change your behavior.

I was at a seminar probably twenty-five years ago, and I listened to a speaker who made a statement that I have never forgotten. He said, "I've never met a lazy person, just one that wasn't properly motivated." He told stories for the next hour about people he had actually known. For example, one young man seemed to be going nowhere until he met the right girl. He then got married, got a better job, and eventually became the president of a company. After every story, he would say that person wasn't lazy, he just hadn't found a way to be properly motivated.

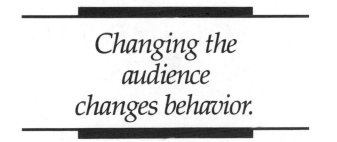

*Changing the audience changes behavior.*

The point is that the individuals had found a new au-

157

dience who believed in them, so they believed in themselves. Therefore, they were able to achieve goals, become presidents, make millions. They went from having no audience to having an audience who believed in them.

So your question becomes, Who was my audience as a child? What did I need from my audience? Did I need my audience to love me? to appreciate me? to make me secure?

If your father was your main audience as a child, your father or older men are the most likely audience to have as an adult. But who is your audience today, and do you need to change that?

For you to change and heal a lot of hurts and traumas you have had in the past you may need to change your audience—from one club to another club or from one friend to another friend or from friends to God. You may be getting negative reinforcement that is keeping the hurt alive. Another audience may be able to help you outgrow that hurt and grow beyond it.

## *Heart of Hearts Reflection*

Ask yourself, Who is my real audience? Who would I like my audience to be?

## 9. Forgive and Ask Forgiveness

Forgiving parents for hurts they've caused stops a lot of bitterness and resentment, which burn up energy at an incredible rate, cause health problems, and may lead to an early grave.

Asking for forgiveness can sometimes resolve hurts and let them heal. But don't go to your children and say, "Here are all the things I did wrong. Please forgive me." That's too much. At least balance your scorecard by saying, "Here are the things I think I did right or tried to do right, and here are some of the things I know I did wrong. Would you please forgive me for that and any hurt it caused you?"

Sometimes parents need to forgive children for hurtful things they have said in the heat of a moment. Sometimes children need to forgive parents for abuses intended or not intended. Sometimes siblings need to forgive siblings for hurts caused by names called and meanness given. Sometimes friends need to forgive friends for lies told and wrongs done.

## 10. Seek Professional Help

You can seek a wise friend or a pastor or a paraprofessional. You can also seek professional help. There are a few times when it is definitely wise to seek professional help:

- When in major depression or feeling suicidal.
- When concerned you may endanger others.

159

- When you feel completely out of control.
- When you can't control substance abuse.

If you're in a backup style and are thinking about suicide or are so deep into drug or substance abuse you can't get out, call 1-800-NEW-LIFE for help. (See Appendix 2.)

These ten steps have brought many tears of healing over the years to me, my friends, and my clients. May the same be true for you and those you love!

Chapter 9

---

# Accepting the Hurts
# That Won't Heal

Some things in life heal very, very slowly, and other things do not or cannot heal. The following principles can help in accepting the hurts that won't heal.

## Step 1:  Realize That It Is 100 Percent Okay Not to Have Your Needs Met 100 Percent of the Time

Things will never be perfect in this life. You are not going to die if your dominant emotional need is not met. It's painful, but you *can* survive.

# Step 2: Get and Keep a Broader Perspective

Always see the one very painful item you may be dealing with in the context of all of the things in your life that are positive.

## Keep Dreams, Goals, and Plans Updated

Use future plans to help you gain a broader perspective on your life than those things in your past that won't heal.

## Start a Positive Progress List

Making a list of what you've done right gives you a needed reminder and reassurance that you're actually making progress in the right direction. It is especially beneficial when you have a devastating failure in one area.

## Make a List of Your Lifelong Friends and Acquaintances

Many times I've talked with clients who have said in a discouraged, lonely tone of voice, "I don't feel I have any friends."

This list can remind you that you have many friends, even though they may be a distance away today and a long time has lapsed since you were together.

# Step 3: Learn a Few Positive Human Nature Assumptions That Are Helpful in Accepting Life's Realities

## Everyone Needs to Give and Receive Love

If you know people who don't seem to, it's because they don't know how to at the moment. Every single person wants to give and receive love.

## Everyone Wants to Grow Personally

All people want to be stronger and more capable this year than they were last year.

## No One Wants to Fail

But a lot of people don't know how to succeed.

## People Do What Makes Sense to Them

They do what makes sense, even though later, it may not make any sense at all.

## Parents Do the Best They Know How

Parents don't want to hurt their children, even though they may not know how to help them. The reality is, your parents may not have known how to raise you any better because their backgrounds or emotional ages made them inadequate parents. Hurts of history are far easier to accept when you see that your parents didn't intentionally hurt you.

# Step 4: You Are God's Student, Not Life's Victim

When Denny Bellesi, the senior pastor of Coast Hills Community Church in Laguna Niguel, California, first stated this idea in a message, it really made sense. It is a fundamental piece of accepting what's happening to us.

Remember, God has us all in school. You aren't life's victim, but you're God's student if you choose to see it that way. You're still under construction.

Steve Arterburn expresses a similar thought: "The question is not, Why did God allow this to happen? Remember He allowed His chosen people to wander in the wilderness. The question is, How can God use it?"

# Step 5: Compete Only with Yourself

Don't compete with your parents, your siblings, or your peers. If you try to compete with others, you will often feel inadequate. But if you compete with yourself, you can begin to make some progress.

# Step 6: Realize That You Can't Win 'Em All

My father Bob Biehl, who lives in Mancelona, Michigan, uses this "nutshell" to accept what he can't change. Whenever Dad runs into something that he finds painful or a tremendous loss or disappointment, he absorbs the loss by saying, "You can't win 'em all."

And he also frequently quotes the truth of Romans 8:28: "And we know that all things work together for good to those who love God, to those who are the called according to His purpose."

If you can't heal hurts in your history, these principles can help in accepting those things that cannot be changed.

# *Heart of Hearts Reflection*

What are the hurts of your past that won't seem to heal, that you simply need to accept? Make a list and consider each one again using the previous six steps.

Chapter 10

---

# Preventing Emotional Damage to Your Children and Grandchildren

Over the past twenty years I have listened to the pain and the pleasures of literally hundreds of executives. I have listened with great interest to hundreds of childhood experiences and their obvious impact on adulthood.

In light of these experiences, let me suggest actions you can take as a parent and actions you can take with your children to help them get ready to be successful and significant adults. I'll also discuss steps to take advantage of a grandparent's unique position.

## Five Proactive Preventative Steps for You as a Parent

### 1. Remove Your Emotional Caps

A high percentage of any damage you may be doing to your children today is caused by the unresolved damage in your life. For example, if you feel inadequate, giving your children a sense of adequacy is very difficult. If you don't feel unconditionally loved, giving them unconditional love is more difficult.

Dealing with your unresolved past (as suggested in chapters 8 and 9) is a gift to your children, a gift of prevention!

For a more complete understanding of how to go about removing emotional caps, see Appendix 1:5.

## 2. Don't Try to Be a Perfect Parent

Being a perfect parent is not only an impossibility, but trying to achieve it puts pressure on you that is unintentionally passed on to the children. Maintain your standards. Keep trying to be a really great parent, but don't put yourself into a perfectionistic parent pressure cooker! (See Appendix 1:7.)

## 3. Keep Your Marriage Strong and Healthy

Know your dominant emotional needs and those of your spouse. Meet each other's needs as consistently as possible.

A familiar and wise saying goes like this: "One of the very finest gifts you can give your child is parents with a great marriage!" I agree 100 percent!

## 4. Avoid Using Your Backup Style on or Around Your Children

If you must use your backup style, use your adult friends as the target. They are big enough and mature enough to protect themselves. Don't vent your frustrations on your children.

See your children as friends, and do not do to them what you would not do to a person you wanted to keep as a lifelong friend. If you wouldn't lose your temper with a friend, why would you lose it with your eight-year-old daughter or son?

### 5. Avoid Certain Behaviors at All Costs

*Abusive behavior*   If you sense that you *may possibly be* abusing your children, ask a close mature friend for objective perspective, or seek counsel from a professional.

*Conditional love*   If you love your children without conditions, tell them so! Tell your children in words, on a regular basis, that you love them.

> *Children don't really feel that they are loved unless they are told they are loved in words.*

*Favoritism between your children*   Some parents feel they are doing children a favor by telling them they are the favorite over their brother(s) and/or sister(s). But that's not so!

A child favored by a parent feels a lot of pressure from peers and frequently gets shut out socially as "Mama's boy" or "Daddy's girl." As much as humanly possible, love and treat your children equally.

*Impossible or constantly changing expectations* One of the most common frustrations I have heard about parents from adult executives is, "I could never do enough to please my parents, or just when I thought I had done it right, the rules changed!"

As much as possible, help your children set goals they can reach with a little stretch. And once a goal has been set or an assignment given, don't change the "deal."

# Eight Preventative Steps to Take with Your Children

## 1. Love Each Child Unconditionally

Tell your child so in words and show him with hugs, pats, kisses, and positive pet names! And whatever you do, do not make these expressions of love conditional on

- cleaning the bedroom perfectly.
- winning the ball game.
- getting straight *A*'s.
- not embarrassing Mom and Dad in public.

When your daughter is chosen to be a cheerleader, tell her you love her just as much as if she had not been chosen. If she is *not* chosen, tell her you love her just as much as if she *had* been chosen!

## 2. Look for the Way in Which Each Child Is Special

Tell the child that she is special, destined for greatness (if you feel that is true). Help the child grow in areas where you feel she is especially gifted.

Look for ways that the child is special—analytical, expressive, artistic, athletic, academic—and tell the child that you can easily see the day when he will one day be great.

## 3. Notice the Individuality of Each Child

Help each child feel important to you personally. You like her or him!

Whenever a child enters the room, always speak the child's name. The smaller the child, the more a pet name is appropriate. This lets the child know that you are noticing that he is important, needed, and noticed.

## 4. Appreciate What Your Child Does Right

Let your child feel he has done it perfectly on occasion. Notice the pure motive with which he baked the mud pie, not that it got your suit dirty!

Get excited about what a child does for you. Tell

172

her what a good job she has done (for her age and ability level). Focus on how much of the room she *did* clean and not just the one or two pieces left unattended.

## Be a cheerleader more than a critic!

### 5. Create a Sense of Security

Show your child how much you love your spouse. Tell him you plan to be married forever (if it is true). Help him *feel* safe and protected in a stable home. If you are already divorced or are anticipating a separation, give your child constant verbal reassurance that you still love him very much. Give him written love notes reassuring him that you love him. And provide for his continued financial security.

Whenever you sense a child is insecure, stop and talk to her and reassure her. If she hears that the economy is bad and that people where you work may be laid off, reassure her that you have a savings account to bridge the gap. Some children need far more security than others. Every child should live in a world where he or she feels secure.

## 6. Respect Each Child as a Person

View each child as a human being. Allow each child a degree of privacy, a degree of secrecy. Remember this child will someday be an adult (this advice is easy for me since my "small" children are now young adults ages twenty-four and twenty-seven). You want to have a relationship of mutual respect with each one at that time. Start now!

Respect for a child can be shown in many little ways. For example, always knock before entering the bedroom, bathroom, or playroom. Don't interrupt him while he is speaking. Be careful not to use your physical size to intimidate and dominate him.

## 7. Help Your Child with Social Adjustment

Help your child choose friends wisely while she is young. Help her see that it takes a certain amount of time and energy to maintain those friendships. Sometimes she needs a little extra guidance, perspective, and understanding.

Sometimes a child needs to take the leadership with a younger child. Sometimes a child needs to play with older children and follow their leadership. And sometimes a child needs to play with friends of the same age. In all of these ways of relating, your child will learn skills to carry into adulthood. She will learn to follow where appropriate and to lead as appropriate.

If you sense that your child is not accepted by other children, or that your child has no friends you would want him to relate to, consider talking with an advisor about how to help him. Consider whatever move necessary to get him into a group you approve of where your child can be an accepted part of the group.

> *Make sure, where possible, that the child relates to same-age friends, to older children, and to younger children.*

## 8. Teach Values You Want Your Child to Carry into Adulthood

Never forget the critical nature of taking time to teach a child the very basic skills of loving, living, and relating. Teach her the values of God, family, country, honesty, fairness, loyalty, courage, and so on.

Have your child memorize key truths. In all of your efforts, recognize that he learns as much or more by watching you as by listening to you. Take him with you where appropriate to learn from you by watching you.

# Three Preventative Steps to Take Advantage of a Grandparent's Unique Position

Actually, a grandparent can help meet all of the needs the parent meets but from a slightly different relationship:

- Love each grandchild unconditionally.
- Look for the way in which each grandchild is special.
- Notice the individuality of each grandchild.
- Appreciate what they do right.
- Create a sense of security.
- Respect each grandchild as a person.
- Help your grandchildren with their social adjustment.
- Teach your grandchildren the values you want them to carry into adulthood. Both by your words and your modeling!

There are three additional steps that you may find helpful from a grandparent's unique position.

## 1. To Prevent Damage to Your Grandchildren, Resolve Any Problem with Their Parents

As Steve Arterburn says, "Those problems we don't resolve, we reproduce in our relationships and especially with our relatives." If you have an unresolved relationship with your son or daughter, now is the time to get it resolved if at all possible!

If you carry any resentment concerning your children, settle it now! If you feel guilty about anything in your past relationship with your children, settle it now! If you have a broken relationship in any way, settle it now!

You know the implications of this saying without elaborate explanations:

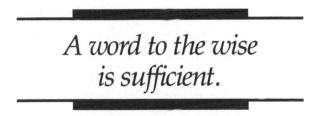

*A word to the wise is sufficient.*

### 2. You May Have More Time to Invest in Your Grandchildren Than Your Children Have at This Point in Their Lives

During these very special times with the grandchildren, keep looking for unique ways they are special, and help your children see just how special their children are in very specific terms.

Some of these times are ideal "break times" for your children when their patience is wearing very thin with the grandchildren.

### 3. Be a Cheerleader for All of the Things Your Children Do Right with Your Grandchildren

All parents need to hear what they are doing right and that they are going to make it. Use your broader, more objective perspective to spot what your children are doing right, and then tell them so in very positive and very specific terms. Don't just say, "You're doing a great job!" Say something like, "You're doing a wonderful job with showing Susie (or Tommy) how to play baseball! You are a great parent!" (You may also want to review Appendix 1:7. "False Parental Guilt.")

These lists are not intended to be exhaustive on the topic of *prevention*. They are meant to suggest some of the most fundamental starting points.

## *Heart of Hearts Reflection*

As you finish this book, I suggest that you reflect carefully on the following:

1. Review your

- "why pattern."
- "Why You Do What You Do" chart.
- Heart of Hearts Reflections.

178

Make any final changes you feel would bring a more precise understanding of your childhood or adulthood.

2. Take Action. Read, gain insight, apply, and *act!*

3. Read Appendix 1 carefully for more insight into why you do what you do.

4. Mark your calendar for an appropriate time in the future when you will again review these areas and your progress toward emotional health and balance.

---

If you have had many "Aha!" experiences and can see clearly where the insights in this book can help you for the rest of your life . . . mission accomplished!

# Appendix 1

---

# Twenty-One Practical Implications and Applications of Why You Do What You Do

This section contains a wide variety of observations that explain in more depth why people do what they do. These topics are listed alphabetically for easy reference.

# 1. Agenda

*Have you ever wondered why you always tend to set the agenda no matter where you go or why you never set the agenda but respond to another person's or the group's agenda?*

When you were a child, who set the agenda? Did you set the agenda, or did someone else? Did you typically lead, did you follow, or was it a combination of both? Neither is right or wrong . . . just different.

Chances are in the 60 to 80 percent range that you have the very same pattern as an adult that you did on the playground in the third or fourth grade.

As a child, were you primarily self-centered or others-centered?

*A self-centered child* tends to set the agenda: It's my agenda, I want to go here, and I assume others will follow; I decide what games we play; I decide who we play with.

*An others-centered child* tends to wait for other people to set the agenda: I don't care. What do you want to do? I'll go with you. What do you want to play?

As an adult, you're going to find for the most part that you feel most comfortable paralleling your childhood role. If you set the agenda as a child, you will likely set the agenda now. If you tended to go along and be supportive of other people, as an adult, you probably tend to go along and be supportive of other people today. Again, not good or bad . . . but different.

A subtle distinction here is the distinction between egotistical and egocentric. An *egotistical* person has a big ego that needs to be stroked all the time. An *egocentric* person assumes that he or she is the center of things.

Some children grow up in a household where their parents are the center of things, and the children are like satellites. Other children grow up where they are the center of things, and their parents are satellites.

If you were raised in a family where your parents and

your siblings revolved around you, as an adult, you will tend to be an *egocentric person* who automatically sets the agenda and assumes other people will follow.

If you grew up in a family where you were one of many and you basically fit into other people's plans, as an adult, your tendency is to wait for a strong person to come along and set an agenda. Then you try to help where you can.

*In your life, who sets the agenda?*

# 2. Assumptions

*Have you ever wondered why you find it so difficult to objectively see your parents' role in your childhood with adult eyes? You may have made one of five* **emotionally dangerous assumptions** *as a child, and they may still be hurting you today.*

An assumption is what you believe to be true, whether or not it is actually true. In some cases your assumptions are true, and in some cases they are not. Either way, you base your behavior on them.

### Dangerous Assumption 1: My Parents Are Perfect; Therefore, I Must Be the Real Problem

I've known a lot of men and women executives who assumed as children that their parents were perfect. If your father was an alcoholic and was never home without yelling at you and your mother and beating you both physically, but you assumed he was perfect, you

184

will feel that you must have done something to cause the problem.

That is a dangerous assumption because as an adult, you come to realize that no parent was ever perfect.

Some parents were inadequately equipped to be wise, loving, balanced parents. Most parents were teenagers in biologically adult bodies trying the best way they knew at the moment to cope with kids.

But if the child assumes that his parents are perfect and he is imperfect, the child assumes responsibility for all problems. This assumption is understandable from a child's perspective.

If that was your view as a child, as an adult, you will want to consciously take a realistic view of your parents as they actually were. Mentally calling your parents by their first names often helps. Your parents were not perfect. They may have been inadequate as parents. They may have had severe problems they were dealing with at the time.

## Dangerous Assumption 2: Mom and Dad Are Healthy, Balanced, Mature Adults Emotionally

Your parents may have been three to thirteen years old emotionally during your junior high and senior high years.

I'll never forget talking with a client who said, "My dad never came through for me. In high school I asked him about girls, and he never came through. In college I asked him about majors, and my dad never came through for me."

I said, "Tell me about your dad."

He said, "Well, when he was *eight*, his mother died."

And I said, "Stop right there. How often do you see your dad?"

He said, "Well, I'm going to see him next week."

"How old is your dad?"

"He's sixty-seven."

I said, "You have a son who's eight, right?"

"Yes."

I said, "When you see your dad next week, call him Dad. But treat him like an emotional eight-year-old and see what happens. If it doesn't work, if he doesn't seem to be responding, stop doing it. But treat him like an eight-year-old emotionally."

He came back two weeks later and said, "Bobb, you're not going to believe it. I asked my son and my father, 'Do you want to go to the store with me?' Both said at the same time, 'Yeah, can we?' I took them to the store, and they were like two little boys. I've never had such a great time with my dad. I had the proper level of expectations—an emotional eight-year-old—and he was very happy."

I then encouraged him to take the logic one step further. "Imagine a teenager coming to your eight-year-old son and asking, 'Hey, how should I treat girls? What about this sex thing?' What would your son tell him at eight years old? 'Well, I don't know.' He wouldn't come through for the teenager, right?

"What if a college student came to your eight-year-old son and said, 'Hey, what major should I choose?'

Your eight-year-old son would look at him as if to say, 'I don't know. Why are you asking me?' That's the way your dad was looking at you."

Assuming that your dad and mother were emotionally mature adults may be a very dangerous emotional assumption. Maybe your dad was ten years old emotionally, and by the time you were in high school, you were already older than he was emotionally. So, don't assume that your dad and mom were mature adults. They may have been emotionally mature, but they may not have been.

### Dangerous Assumption 3: Everyone Is Like Me

*Everyone is not like you.*

- You may be original in your creativity, but others may be adaptive in their creativity.
- You may like new projects all the time, but others may want low risk and no new projects.
- You may want to be captain of everything, but others don't want to be captain of anything.

Not everyone is like you by design. Assuming that other people are just like you is dangerous.

### Dangerous Assumption 4: When I Grow Up, I'm Destined to Be Just Like Mom or Dad

When you grow up, you may be very different from either or both of your parents. They may love (what seems to you like) an extremely boring level of routine; you may always need and want a new challenge and change. They may have a very high need for control; you may get excited only when it seems that things are almost out of control. They may be adaptively creative; you may be originally creative.

### Dangerous Assumption 5: If I Don't Please Mom and Dad, I'm a Failure

Well, that isn't necessarily true. They may have wanted something for you that was wrong for you; they may have wanted something for you that they wanted for themselves and put it on you, but that never fit you at all. Just because your dad was a successful farmer and you're an artist doesn't mean that you're a failure.

# 3. Conflict Resolution

*Have you ever wondered why conflict is so stressful for you and why you tend to withdraw from it, or possibly, on the other hand, why you seek conflict?*

How did you see your parents resolving conflict? You will tend to resolve conflict as an adult today similar to the way your parents modeled it for you years ago.

One of my clients, a very successful business executive, said, "Whenever it came to conflict, my father just shut up and left the room. As a matter of fact, I never once saw him actually deal with conflict in any way. Today, I *do not know* how to deal with conflict."

188

Constant fighting between parents may have had a tremendously damaging impact on you as a child. You may say, "I don't ever want to fight." So you avoid conflict as an adult. Or you may have seen your dad or your mom always win every argument. The pattern you feel most comfortable with in dealing with conflict is most likely the one you saw your mom or dad use.

That pattern may not be the one you *choose* to use as an adult, but your first intuitive, automatic response will be to approach the conflict like the parent with which you identified most strongly. If you solve it differently, you've consciously learned how to confront differently.

# 4. Deceased Loved Ones

*Have you ever wondered why your deceased parent still has so much control over you and your behavior, for good or for bad?*

Some of us have been influenced, supported, encouraged, and loved by people who have passed away. And we never said, "Thank you."

There is nothing preventing you from taking flowers, sitting at the grave side, and having an hour's conversation. I am certainly *not* suggesting that you try to talk to the person's spirit or anything. Just pretend the person is there and say out loud what you have come to see as an adult. You can express feelings of appreciation you would want to express if the person was alive to hear you.

Expressing these insights (positive and negative) can be a resolving experience. Don't be afraid of tears.

Recently, a client took his father to the grave of a couple who had raised him as a child. The father could not remember ever thanking them. The last time he had seen them was fifty years ago. When he went to their graves, he took flowers and talked to them with many, many tears for over two hours.

He expressed how much he appreciated that though they were not his parents, they were the only ones he remembered giving him unconditional love. The experience relieved, resolved, cured, salved, soothed, and healed something deep in his being that may not have been healed in any other way.

So if you've got an aunt or an uncle or a grandparent or someone from your childhood, seriously consider taking flowers to the grave and sitting and talking to the person's memory.

This process can also help take the emotional pain out of some conflicts you had with parents that can never be resolved in other ways.

# 5. Emotional Caps

*Have you ever wondered why it is so hard for you to feel like a mature adult? Have you ever felt that you were incapable of an adult-adult relationship?*

Let's say your mother died when you were eight years old, and the experience was traumatic. You haven't disclosed how you really feel about things since you were eight years old. How do you go about telling people that? How do you grow past eight years old?

How do you remove those caps on emotional development? The only way I've ever seen to do it is to get into a relationship with someone you are convinced loves you unconditionally. Then you go back and emotionally experience what you experienced at that age, whether it's rage or fear or anxiety. Experience it as though you were seven or eight years old, and have that person still love and accept you.

You almost instantly seem a year or two older emotionally. Then you're nine or ten. The problem is that if you had trauma at eight years old and you resolve it, you're going to have to process the traumas you experienced at nine, ten, eleven, and so on. Basically, you will have to keep processing traumas through each year until you are the same age emotionally as you are physically.

# 6. Emotional Masks

*Have you ever wondered why you feel such pressure to appear to be something you are not? Frequently, this pressure results in emotional masks and capped or stunted emotional growth.*

As I've studied the three selves model that I explained early in this book, and I've interacted with people about it, I've concluded that many people have experienced a lot of hurt and a lot of pressure to appear to be something they're not.

> *The minute you put on a mask of "I'm happy" when you are really sad or "I'm not afraid" when you are really terrified, you stop growing emotionally.*

Your ability to relate to other people in regard to who you really are stunts at that point; it stops growing; it ends. Only as you can share with another human being what's going on inside you can you begin to grow again relationally and emotionally and express who you really are.

### An Athlete Mask

Many executives I have worked with started wearing an athlete mask when they were four to ten years old.

They put on that mask and have never felt like anything but an athlete. That's the only way they know how to relate to people.

Many don't know how to relate to people as adults at all. They are socially gracious but in terms of exposing who they really are to someone else, they are totally incapable of relating to a person in a mode other than conversations like these:

- "How big is your boat? Mine is bigger."
- "What kind of a car do you drive? I got a new one last month."
- "How many cars do you have?"
- "How many condominiums do you have?"

That's what I call *mask matching*. Mask matchers rarely speak in terms like these:

- "Are you ever afraid that all this is going to evaporate and you're going to be left homeless?"
- "Do you ever feel like just groaning at night because you are so lonely?"
- "Do you ever feel afraid that your spouse is going to leave you?"

That level of buddy talk, done with a close friend where you're exposing what is really in your heart, who you really are, what you're really experiencing, never happens. Communication is mask-to-mask, shell-to-shell, public self-to-public self.

If people have one or two close friends they can really open up to, confide in, and trust, they are fortunate.

Other people I know put on professional masks, corporate masks, or academic masks. When a person starts wearing the doctor or broker mask, suddenly there are no real relationships. Getting beyond the mask to sharing about the personal self is extraordinarily difficult.

### A Family Mask

A family can put on a mask or project a public image. A few examples: "Our family has no real problems." "Our family is in no pain from an alcohol problem." "Our family is made up of only winners." "Our family is the perfect Leave-it-to-Beaver family."

Can you imagine the amount of pressure on any one member who is less than a perfect upholder of the family image and the family name?

## 7. False Parental Guilt

*Have you ever wondered why you feel so guilty about the past with your children and if you are being too hard on yourself? Here are some ways to deal with the false guilt you may be feeling.*

## Distinguish Between False Guilt and Real Guilt

Be quick to ask forgiveness for the things you did that you know hurt them, whether you meant to at the time or not. Perfectionistic parents suffer from false guilt because they were not perfect. Consider asking a close friend for an objective perspective on how you did, or are doing, as a parent.

## Admit That No Parent Is Perfect

Admit up front, "I made (or will make) mistakes." Parents are not perfect . . . just human! Let the kids see that *you* are not perfect.

## Remember That You Did a Lot of Things Right

Make a list of the things you did right. You did the best you could at the time. You didn't have all of the answers then that you have now. Tell your older children that you hope they can do a better job than you did when they become parents.

## Encourage Your Adult Children to Read This Book

Talk over some of the issues adult-to-adult.

## Accept That Children Eventually Must Be Responsible for Their Acts

By their teen years, your children will make their own major decisions, some good, some bad. They need to learn to deal with the direct consequences of their decisions. And that is not always easy on parents.

### Help Your Children See That They Are God's Students, Not Life's Victims

You may want to refer to the discussion in chapter 9 about this idea.

### Pray for Them Constantly

Tell them that you are praying for them—and why.

### Ask for Perspective from a Nonfamily Member

Ask a mentor or friend for parenting help and support.

### Take Initiative

Tell your children that you love them unconditionally! Even though some of their actions have dire consequences, you still love them. Tell them that you are proud of what they are doing right. Don't point out just where they are not measuring up to your standards.

### Encourage Them to Seek Professional Help

If they have multiple predominantly negative childhood feelings, consider encouraging them to see a professional counselor. Offer to go with them.

# 8. Fear of Becoming Just Like a Parent

*Have you ever wondered why you are so afraid of becoming just like your mom or dad and what you can do to avoid it?*

## Run a Reality Check

You are *not* just like your parent. You have had

- different parents.
- different models growing up.
- different homes.
- different aunts and uncles.
- different decades in which to grow up.
- different friends who influenced you.
- different schools and instructors.
- different opportunities to grow.
- different spouses.
- different financial situations.

And these are just a few of the differences!

Make your own more complete list of the differences between you and your parents for a reminder and reassurance at key points.

## Focus on Strengths of Your Parent

Be careful not to focus on the weakness that you want to avoid. You may have to ask siblings, grandparents, aunts and uncles, and friends to help you create such a list of strengths of each parent. You may currently see them with negative eyes.

### Choose a Healthy New Model of Adulthood

Choose someone you want to be more like; watch the person closely. Avoid watching only your parent, focusing on what you do *not* want to become.

### Risk

Candidly admit to your spouse your fear of becoming "just like Mom or Dad." Enroll your spouse in the process of helping you grow beyond your parental modeling. Urge your spouse not to use this new information as an ultimate weapon in the middle of an argument, for example, saying, "You are just like your mom (or dad)!"

### Ask a Mentor or Friend for Help

A nonfamily member can offer a unique perspective on the situation. And in many cases, a mentor or friend can be a healthy model for you.

### Study the Reasons for Your Parent's Behavior

It is easier to escape the fear of becoming like someone by understanding how the person came to be who he or she is. Interview grandparents, aunts, uncles, and friends. How did (do) they see your parent? Ask your parent to read this book, and then discuss the situation adult-to-adult.

## Recognize That Healthy Models Have Already Contributed to Your Personal Development

You may want to take the additional step of seeking them out and thanking them for their positive influence in your life.

## Mentally Call Your Parents by Their First Name

Doing this helps you consistently see them with adult eyes. You have an opportunity to adjust expectations of your parent as a person, not just as a parent!

## Develop a Totally Different Image from Your Parent

Work at consciously developing an image that is yours.

- Dress differently.
- Comb your hair differently.
- Live in a different place.
- Do different work.
- Go to a different church.
- Join a different club.

## Seek Professional Help

If you feel you are losing ground and you are becoming more like a parent—especially if the modeling included immoral, illegal, or unethical behavior—seek help from a professional. (For guidelines on deciding on a treatment center, see Appendix 2.)

# 9. Home

*Have you ever wondered why two kids raised in the same home turned out so differently? NO TWO CHILDREN ARE EVER RAISED IN THE SAME HOME! Even identical twins are not raised in the same home emotionally speaking.*

Parents can tell immediately which is by nature "more like your side of the family" or "more like my side of the family," or which "takes after you" or "is more like me." And each twin is treated ever so slightly different by the father and by the mother.

And once you move beyond identical twins, the differences are even easier to identify. Every year has certain struggles and strengths, losses and gains in it. Some years are better than others. Sometimes parents are grieving the loss of a loved one, loss of a job, or physical problems. All of these factors change life.

Let's say when you were in the fourth grade, your dad wasn't making much money, and you lived in a small house. But when your younger sister or brother was in the fourth grade, your parents were in a different financial or social status. The home was different emotionally speaking.

Then if one child—because of hair color (runs in Dad's family), family resemblance, or any other unspoken reality, preference, or prejudice—felt special to the father but not the mother, that child does not grow up the same as the child who felt rejected by the parent. The home was different emotionally speaking.

For some people recognizing that has been an "aha!" experience.

# 10. "I Feel" List

*1. Circle each word that expresses an emotion you are currently feeling.*
*2. Double circle those you feel more intensely.*
*3. Star the top ten you feel most intensely.*
*4. Double star the top three emotions you are experiencing.*
*5. Triple star the number one dominant emotion you are currently experiencing.*

| | |
|---|---|
| Abandoned | Alert |
| Abused | Alienated |
| Admired | Alive |
| Adored | Alone |
| Affectionate | Amazed |
| Affirmed | Ambivalent |
| Afraid | Amused |
| Aggressive | Angry |
| Alarmed | Annoyed |

Antagonistic

Anticipating

Anxious

Apathetic

Appealing

Appreciated

Apprehensive

Approved

At ease

Attractive

Awed

Awkward


Bad

Baffled

Bashful

Battered/
  Bruised

Behind

Belittled

Benevolent

Betrayed

Bewildered

Bitter

Bored

Bound

Brave

Brilliant

Broke

Buried

Burned out


Callous

Capable

Cared for

Challenged

Cheated

Claustrophobic

Comfortable

Committed

Competitive

Concerned

Confident

Confused

Consoled

Content

Courageous

Creative

Cynical


Daring

Defeated

Defensive

Degraded

Dejected

Delighted

Dependent

Depressed

Despair

Despised

Destined

Determined

Devastated

Disappointed

Disciplined

Discontented

Disgusted

Dishonest

Disillusioned

Disloyal

Dismal

Dismayed

Disorganized

Disoriented

Dissatisfied

Down and out

Drifting

Driven

Drowning

Dry

Dumb


Eager

Edgy

Effective

Efficient

Elated

Embarrassed

Empty

Enchanted

Enthusiastic

Envious

Esteemed

Estrangement

Excited

Exhausted

Failure

Faithful

Fatherless

Fatigued

Fearful

Fed up

Focused

Foggy

Foolish

Forgiving

Forlorn

Fragmented

Free

Friendly

Frightened

Frustrated

Fulfilled

Fun focused

Furious

Futile

Generous

Glad

Gloomy

Good

Graceful

Gratified

Great

Guilty

Handcuffed

Happy

Hated

Hectic

Held back

Helpless

Hollow

Honest

Honored

Hopeful

Hopeless

Horrified

Hostile

Humiliated

Hyper

Idolized

Ignored

Impatient

Important

Inadequate

Incapable

Included

Indecisive

Independent

Indifferent

Indignant

Ineffective

Inexperienced

Infatuated

Inferior

Influential

Infuriated

Inhibited

Insecure

Insignificant

Inspired

Intelligent

Interested

Intimidated

Irritated

Isolated

Jealous

Jolly

Joyful

Left behind

Lethargic

Like a nobody

Liked

Listless

Loathed

Lonely

Lost

Loved

Loyal

Lustful

Mad

Mismatched

Misplaced

Misunderstood

Mixed up

Moody

Naive

Negative

Neglected

Nervous

Nicheless

Numb

Obnoxious

Old

On track

Optimistic

Optionless

Out of control

Out of shape

Overcommitted

Overweight

Overwhelmed

Pain

Panicky

Passed by

Passionate

Patient

Peaceful

Perplexed

Pitied

Pleased

Popular

Positive

Pressured

Professional

Progress

Prosperous

Protected

Proud

Provoked

Puzzled

Ragged

Ready

Regret

Rejected

Relaxed

Relieved

Reluctant

Resentment

Resigned

Resistant

Respected

Responsible

Restless

Revengeful

Sad

Satisfied

Scared

Scattered

Secure

Self-conscious

Sensitive

Sexy

Shame

Shocked

Shuffled

Shy

Sick

Significant

Smart

Smothered

Stable

Stagnant

Stifled

Streetwise

Stretched

Strong

Stunned

Stunted

Successful

Sullen

Superior

Sure

Suspicious
Sympathetic

Teachable
Tempted
Tender
Tense
Tentative
Terrified
Threatened
Timid
Tired
Torn up
Trapped
Treadmilled
Turned on

Unappreciated
Unattractive
Uncertain
Uncomfortable
Understaffed
Underpaid

Undereducated
Underrated
Undisciplined
Undiscovered
Unfaithful
Unhappy
Unheard
Unlimited
Unloved
Unneeded
Unpopular
Unprofessional
Unsexy
Unsure
Unwanted
Unwise
Upset
Used
Useless

Valiant
Venturesome
Vibrant

| | |
|---|---|
| Wanted | Worried |
| Warm | Worthless |
| Washed up | Worthy |
| Weak | Wrongly |
| Weary | accused |
| Weepy | |
| Wise | Yearning |
| Withdrawn | |
| Worn out | Zealous |

# 11. Loneliness

*Have you ever wondered why you feel so lonely even when you are with close friends? There are actually several kinds of loneliness.*

## Professional Loneliness

You are alone in your profession. You may have a lot of friends at church. You may have lots of social friends. But professionally, no one else may be working on the kinds of projects you're working on.

## Financial Loneliness

You are the only one who knows you're in financial trouble, and you can't share it with anyone. Or you may have just earned a huge bonus, but telling all of your friends would intimidate them.

### Spiritual Loneliness

You are the only one who believes as you do in a whole group of people.

### Social Loneliness

This condition is what most people think of when they say, "I feel lonely," meaning they don't currently have social relationships.

### Relational Loneliness

You have friendships, but you don't have anyone with whom you can have a heart-to-heart talk.

So ask yourself, If I am feeling lonely, what kind of loneliness am I feeling?

# 12. Manhood and Womanhood

*Have you ever wondered why you do not feel totally confident as a "real man"?*

### Manhood

How would your father have completed this sentence: "A real man is a man who _____ _____"?

If you choose to define it differently, you're going to

have a certain amount of conflict in your system. Let's say, for example, your dad would have completed it like this: "A real man is a man who milks fifty cows before breakfast."

Your dad grew up on a farm, and that's the way he would have defined manhood. But let's say you're a fine artist and you paint pictures like Van Gogh, Picasso, Degas, Rembrandt, Renoir, or one of the other world-class painters. You may make fifty times what your dad makes in a year.

By all financial standards, you are more successful than your father. Socially, you may be better positioned. Spiritually, professionally, and physically, you may be far more balanced than your father ever dreamed of being.

But if your father defined manhood in terms of milking fifty cows before breakfast, chances are, he has never admitted that you're a man yet. And if he has never admitted it, how do you conclude that you are a man?

I'll never forget watching an interview on television of a screen star. The interviewer asked him, "You're a man, you're a man's man, you're a macho man. When does a man become a man?"

He looked at her. He thought a minute, sort of smiled, and said, "A man becomes a man when his daddy tells him he is and not before."

I thought to myself, *You're smarter than I've given you credit for.* But then about three months later, it was like something exploded in my head, and I thought, *Oh, no, if he is right, we're all in trouble.* I began to think about the number of boys who grew up without fathers.

In working with hundreds of men, I've concluded that many men will never be told they're men because their fathers have never been told by *their* fathers that they are men. As a result, we have a generation of men who don't know if they're men or not.

Your father may never tell you you're a man. If you've chosen in life to go a different way and not to milk fifty cows before breakfast, he may never have the capacity or the eyes to see that you're a grown-up adult man. You will have to conclude in your own way, through another father figure or through your own view of manhood, that you are, in fact, a man.

I work with teams of executive men and have spent a considerable amount of time discussing this topic with them.

---

*Most typically,
one-third of the men
in a group admit
spontaneously that
they've struggled
with their manhood.*

---

May I suggest that until an adult man, someone you respect, respects you as an adult equal, you will not feel your manhood is complete. If your father is incapable of it, you may not really be confident that you are a man until you have a relationship in which you are respected as a man.

Another dimension of manhood is that a man may have had his manhood affirmed only by women. His mother thinks of him as a man and his wife thinks of him as a man, but he feels really uncomfortable with other men because no man has ever told him he is, in fact, an adult man. Our generation is filled with men looking for a mentor, someone who will appropriately say, "You are a man!"

## Womanhood

Frankly, I am not as confident as to how the womanhood issue works. However, I have talked with many women who work with women's issues, and their consensus seems to be that what *man*hood is to men, *mother*hood is to women.

Perhaps a woman who remains childless may remain a child in her mother's eyes.

A common dynamic I have found in working with women is a feeling that their mothers will not accept the fact that they are adults. Possibly the most helpful thing those adult daughters can do is to mentally call their mothers by their first names.

I have actually suggested many times that a daughter and a mother call each other by their first names for a one-hour window of time in order to establish a more adult relationship. In at least a few cases, this has worked well. But I'm confident there are also other relationships where it would not work well at all!

# 13. Meditation and Memory

*Have you ever wondered why your natural line of thinking is so negative and how to work toward a more positive view of the world?*

Before you left home as a teenager, you had as many as 20,000 to 30,000 (6,000 days times 5 impressions per day equals 30,000) emotional impressions of how life really is in the world. As many as 5,000 to 10,000 of those impressions were made before you became a teenager. If thousands of the impressions were very, very negative, you will have a difficult time replacing them with positive ones.

To keep focused on adult truth rather than the emotional impressions from childhood, you may want to reflect often on biblical passages.

Reflect on these passages if you are feeling

| Insignificant | Conditionally Loved |
|---|---|
| Genesis 1:26–27, 31 | Psalm 9:10 |
| Psalm 37:1–6 | Isaiah 43:1 |
| Psalm 39:4–5 | Mark 11:25–26 |

## Insignificant

Psalm 139:13–17

Proverbs 8:21

Proverbs 16:18–20

Proverbs 26:12

John 1:12

1 Corinthians 15:51–54

Galatians 6:7–9

Philippians 3:14–16

Hebrews 13:5

1 Peter 5:7

1 John 2:15–17

## Conditionally Loved

John 3:16

John 14:1–3

John 15:12–16

Romans 5:6–8

Romans 8:14–15

Romans 8:38–39

Galatians 3:26; 4:1–7

1 John 4:9–19

## Loss of Respect

Deuteronomy 5:16

Proverbs 23:24–26

Isaiah 30:18

John 12:42–43

John 15:15

1 Corinthians 2:9

1 Corinthians 4:1–5

2 Corinthians 10:17–18

Galatians 6:9

## Ignored

Psalm 22:24

Psalm 55:22

Matthew 11:28

John 16:23–24

Ephesians 2:3–6

Colossians 3:12

Titus 3:3–5

Hebrews 13:5

1 Peter 5:7

**Loss of Respect**

2 Timothy 1:7
Hebrews 13:6

**Inadequate**

Psalm 73:26
Psalm 127:1–2
Ecclesiastes 3:12–13
Matthew 25:35–40
Mark 9:23
Acts 20:32–35
Galatians 6:9
James 2:15–16
James 5:7–8
2 Peter 1:4

**Intimidated**

Psalm 37
Psalm 42:5–11
Psalm 138:7

**Ignored**

1 John 5:14–15

**Insecure**

Psalm 9:10
Psalm 18:2
Psalm 46:1–3
Psalm 139:7–12
Isaiah 58:9
Matthew 6:25–34
John 14:18–27
John 16:3
Romans 8:15
Romans 8:35–39
Hebrews 13:6
1 John 4:4

**Unacceptable**

Isaiah 43:1
John 14:1–3
John 15:12–16

| **Intimidated** | **Unacceptable** |
|---|---|
| Proverbs 16:7 | Romans 5:6–8 |
| Proverbs 23:17–18 | 2 Corinthians 3:4–6 |
| Jeremiah 39:17–18 | Ephesians 2 |
| Luke 1:74 | Philippians 3:7–16 |
| John 16:33 | Colossians 3:12–14 |
| Romans 10:11 | 1 Peter 2:4–10 |
| 2 Corinthians 5:17 | 1 John 4:9–19 |
| 2 Timothy 1:7 | |

I owe special thanks to Ed Trenner, a senior associate with Masterplanning Group International, for compiling this list of Scriptures.

# 14. Nicknames

*Have you ever wondered why nicknames are so important to you and to others?*

When you give a child a positive pet name or a nickname, the child assumes automatically, "He is speaking to my personal self. He likes me personally." So, when you call a child "pumpkin" or "ducky," the child assumes you are talking to the "real me." And the child feels closer to you.

For nieces, nephews, children, grandchildren, or neighborhood children, think carefully about the nickname you give each child. Give the name in a way that's positive, warm, and loving. Giving a nickname tells the child, "When I use this name with you, I'm talking to the real you that only we know about."

Become a master at giving nicknames and you will do tremendous favors to children of your world.

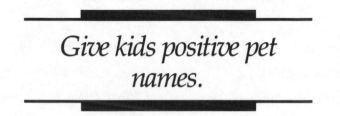

## *Give kids positive pet names.*

You may be saying, "No one ever gave me a nick-name. Why?"

There are a couple of reasons. First, when people have unusual names, others give them nicknames more often. Second, when people have common names, others don't go to the trouble of coming up with something else.

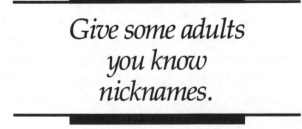

## *Give some adults you know nicknames.*

You might want to ask yourself, Who are the three adults I would most like to communicate with at a

218

heart-to-heart level? If I developed a nickname or a pet name for each one, what would I give? If they never had a nickname, giving them one is a fun experience; it is never too late.

## 15. Parties and Fun!

*Have you ever wondered why you enjoy parties so much and your spouse simply doesn't, or vice versa?*

Of what value, or lack of value, was fun to your family when you were growing up? In some families, parties, fun, and exercise were given no value whatsoever. The extras of life were never to be sought after, never to be appreciated or enjoyed.

Having a social life, relaxing, holding a party or barbecue, inviting friends over, going out to dinner, taking a trip, or going on a vacation was never valued by some and may have been considered a waste of time and money.

You might want to ask yourself, What were the things my family did not value that society or my spouse values a lot? You may find the answers very interesting as an adult. You may find five pieces of your ten-thousand-piece puzzle right here.

## 16. Relationships

*Have you ever wondered why you have only one best friend? Or why you have three best friends you want to hang around with all the time? Or why you are socially gracious to everyone but are really close to no one?*

The most successful (that is, satisfying, comfortable, secure) relationships you had as a child are predictably paralleled in adulthood a high percentage of the time. If you had one best friend in elementary school, you'll likely have one best friend today as an adult. If you were a social loner in elementary school, chances are far above average that you are a social loner today as an adult.

If you were a loner kid, you may be socially gracious today as an adult but relationally unattached. Your interest in having a heart-to-heart conversation with someone may be drastically reduced compared to the person who had two or three really close friends as a child.

Complete this statement: The most satisfying relationships I remember having as a child were with

- adults.
- aunts or uncles.
- big brother or sister.
- buddies (two to four who were always together).
- Father.
- friends in general (friendly to everyone, close to no one).

- grandparents.
- little brother or sister.
- Mother.
- no one (I was a social loner).
- one really close friend.
- the "in" crowd.
- three to four close friends.

# *Heart of Hearts Reflection*

If your most satisfying relationships as a child were with family and other adults, chances are good that today your most satisfying relationships are with your family and older people. If you said that your most satisfying childhood relationships were with peers, siblings, or friends, chances are, you have lots of friends and really enjoy friendships today. If you said that you didn't have any close relationships, chances are, you don't have any today. The parallels are striking.

Another way to think about your relational pattern is to study your emotionally significant relationships. Ask the questions:

> Whose opinion of me most helped shape how I wore my hair, what clothes I wore, or how I saw life as a child?
>
> When I was in the third, fourth, or fifth grade, who most shaped how I looked?
>
> Who decided whether I wanted to see a new movie or not, or what toys I preferred?

The people you wanted to be acceptable to were shaping in terms of who you were as a child. As an adult, you may look back and say about your peers, "Well, I've forgotten their names. They weren't significant emotionally. All of my important relationships were with family members."

Who were the people with whom you had the most satisfying relationships as a child? Get them in mind. Your influences from your childhood relationships are the primary shapers of your view of things such as authority and competition.

Were you competitive as a child? If so, you're competitive as an adult. If you were not competitive as a child, you're probably not competitive as an adult. Whenever you were competing, did you typically win or lose? If you typically won, chances are, you continue today in a friendly sort of way. But if you typically lost, chances are, you don't compete today.

It's helpful to gain an adult perspective of your childhood years to see the role that competition played. For example, if you related mostly to adults for adult recognition, you may have been competitive with your peers for the attention of those adults.

One client said to me, "I was always the favored student by the teacher, I was the favored child by my parents, I was always the adult favorite, so I was always doing things to curry the favor of adults. But it alienated me from my peers. So today I relate a lot to older people. I don't have any friendships except with older people."

Frequently, brothers compete fiercely for the affection and attention of their father. If you competed as a boy for the affection of your father, as an adult, you'll likely compete with your peers for the recognition of your team leader (boss, manager, or supervisor).

## *Beware of too much competition.*

The cold, hard reality is that the more competitive you are as an adult, the fewer close friends you have. If you're always competing fiercely, you likely divide people into two categories: those who can beat you and those you can beat. Those who can beat you intimidate you and those you can beat seem inferior to you. So, who is left to be your friend?

If you have always prided yourself on being extremely competitive, you may need to take a second look and ask, For the next few years, do I want to be known as a competitor, or do I want to be known as a friend?

Sometimes it takes professional help to outgrow your dependence on competitiveness to make you feel good about yourself. On the other hand, if you compete with no one for anything, and you can't stand up to competition, that's another whole area needing growth.

# 17. Role Parallels

*Have you ever wondered why you are always playing the role of captain or are never the captain?*

The role you played as a child is likely the role you are most comfortable playing today as an adult.

These childhood roles are frequently paralleled in adulthood. Complete this statement: The role I remember playing the most as a child was that of a (an)

- academic.
- advisor.

224

- affirmer.
- athlete.
- bookworm.
- bully.
- captain of everything.
- cheerleader or encourager.
- child (to be seen and not heard).
- clown or entertainer.
- competitor for parent's attention.
- computer whiz.
- dutiful daughter.
- egghead.
- gang leader or ringleader.
- happy child.
- life of the party.
- loner.
- music star.
- organizer.
- parent substitute for brothers and/or sisters.
- peacemaker.
- princess.
- producer.
- star student.
- superstar, not the captain.

- tagalong.
- tattletale.
- teacher's pet.
- team player.
- water boy (or girl).
- weakling.

List your primary role(s).

_____

_____

_____

What does all this role parallel theory mean? It *does not* say that you can't be anything. It does not say that you can't be a leader, be in business, or play the role as president of the company. The main point is that the most comfortable roles, the ones that take the least effort for you to play as an adult, are those that are paralleled in childhood.

Another dimension of parallel childhood-adult roles is role reversal. I have one very close friend who always played the role of little brother. His big brother was such an outstanding person, athlete, and leader that the little brother, who had tremendous leadership ability in his own right, went along in his older brother's

226

shadow. He was always with his older brother. The little brother always left the initiative up to the big brother.

Unfortunately, when the big brother was thirty-five years old, he was killed in a freak hunting accident. Now the little brother finds it awkward and uncomfortable to take the initiative.

He is in a position in his company where he has to take the initiative, but he feels like a duck out of water or a turtle on its back. He doesn't feel comfortable in the presidential role. He is actually doing a very good job. But in terms of comfort level, he is always wishing his older brother were there to take the leadership in the situation. It puts a lot of pressure on him.

# 18. Stoic Parents

*Have you ever wondered why you are so sensitive to your entire environment?*

A consistent emotional pattern in children raised by stoic parents is hypersensitiveness to environment. They will constantly look for more and more subtle cues about what individuals are really trying to communicate.

If a parent is outgoing and demonstrative, the child doesn't have to be that sensitive to pick up the communication. But if the parent never changes expression and only changes tone slightly to mean, "I'm about to hit you, I'm mad at you, or I'm upset with you," the child must pick up smaller and smaller signals about what to expect.

Therefore, if you were raised by a stoic parent who was *unpredictably harsh or explosive,* you became hypersensitive not just to a person but to your entire surroundings.

One client stated, "My mother used to sneak around behind me and hit me on the ears." As a result, he is sensitive to absolutely everything in the environment—not only to the person talking to him but to a waitress walking by or to people talking in another booth.

# 19.  Teams

*Have you ever wondered why you are so team oriented or why you never think in terms of being a part of a team? Have you ever wondered why you never assume your team will actually make it to the championships?*

Another dimension of this role-play parallel between childhood and adulthood is the way you experienced teams. Did your teams typically win? Did they typically lose? Or was it fifty-fifty?

The people who make all-pro typically tend to have been on winning teams all the way from childhood to adulthood. And the ones who don't make it or choke in the ninth inning are often adults with childhood patterns that say, "Well, you're not going to win anyway. You'll get up maybe to a winning season, but you won't win the championship."

After growing up on losing teams, becoming part of

a world-class winning team is a difficult thing, mentally and emotionally, even for a gifted athlete.

# 20. Unspoken Family Values

*Have you ever wondered why you tend to look at so many things the way your parents did, even though those issues were never discussed openly?*

What was the highest unspoken family value in your home as a child—to get rich, be popular, or trust no one? There are a few specific areas in which your parents' unspoken family values have influenced your adult behavior in significant ways:

- How you show *affection*
- How you view *authority*
- How you *resolve conflict*
- How you *perceive food*
- How you understand *manhood* and *womanhood* roles
- How you view *money*
- How much you are driven to *performance*
- How you view *parties* and *fun*
- How you see *work* as an adult
- How you view the *country* in which you live and your *civic responsibilities*

## 21. Your Name

*Have you ever wondered why you long to hear your name spoken aloud?*

Some people desperately long to hear their names spoken.

I was at a friend's birthday party. I don't remember how it came up, but the wife turned very angrily to her husband and demanded, "Why don't you ever say my name? Is that too much to ask for you to say my name? Would you please, one time, say my name?"

Most guests stood around aghast, asking silently, "Where did *that* come from?" I knew where it came from.

A person who has felt ignored as a child desperately needs and longs to hear her name spoken. The split second that the name is spoken, the person knows that the speaker is focused completely on her. When her name is spoken, at that moment in time she is not being ignored.

So, whenever you sense that people were ignored in childhood and need attention in adulthood, call them by name as much as you can. They long to, need to, hear the name and receive affirmation of themselves.

Appendix 2

---

# Treatment Centers: Questions You Need to Ask Before You Decide

Asking the right questions and making the best decision about a treatment center may be the difference between beginning a new life of emotional freedom or continuing to be imprisoned by personal pain.

## Is the Facility Accredited by the Joint Commission on Accreditation of Healthcare Organizations (JCAHO)?

Accreditation by this organization means the center is being run in line with quality standards accepted by

Note: This section has been adapted from Stephen Arterburn's entry in *The Question Book* (Nashville: Thomas Nelson, Oliver-Nelson, 1993).

most hospitals and healthcare organizations in the country. Without this, there is a good chance that insurance will not cover the cost of treatment and that standards of care may be lacking.

## How Much Does the Program Cost?

Some programs charge an all-inclusive rate, and some charge by the day. Be sure you know the total expected cost. Doctor's charges are separate from those for the hospital, so ask the staff to break down the charges.

## Does My Insurance Cover the Cost of Care?

Often programs are covered by insurance but not all insurance. You need to give the program your group insurance number so administrators can check on your specific coverage.

## What Should I Do if My Insurance Does Not Cover Treatment?

If your insurance does not cover treatment at that facility, you have to decide whether you will pay for treatment out of your pocket or choose a facility where insurance will approve payment. Is the treatment important enough to your life to make sacrifices to pay for personally?

# Do You Have the Name of Someone Who Has Been Through the Program That I Could Call?

The most vital call could be this one. A person who was treated at the program is proof about whether or not the program is reputable with high standards of quality. Proverbs 20:18 tells us that wise people seek good counsel. Asking someone who has been through the program about the quality of care is the best counsel you can obtain.

## Who Endorses the Program?

If other mental healthcare professionals refer to this program, you might want to call one of them for an endorsement. However, being given a famous name of someone who likes the program could mean very little. That person might be paid to endorse the program. Seek out those who have worked alongside the treatment team to vouch for the quality of care obtained there.

## What Are the Values of the Managers of the Program?

The last thing you want to do is to enter into a program that goes against your values. When people come to New Life Treatment Centers, they know that our program will be consistent with conservative Judeo-Christian values. If you are a Christian and you are put into a secular program, your faith might be attacked as part of the problem. Find a program that incorporates healthy faith into all aspects.

## Are Twelve-Step Groups Provided?

Twelve-Step programs, such as Alcoholics Anonymous, are a must if you are to maintain a long-term recovery. If a facility does not introduce you to this type of group, it is robbing you of no-cost support found throughout the world. If people start working with the Twelve Steps while in treatment, they seem to accept more responsibility for their recovery, and they become less dependent on the therapist over the years.

## Should I Consider Inpatient Hospital Treatment?

Treatment in a hospital—with a full medical staff including doctors, nurses, and a team of professionals in social work, counseling, and psychology—is the most comprehensive treatment and is the most protective environment. You would remain at the facility throughout treatment.

## Is Residential Treatment More Appropriate?

Residential treatment involves a lower level of care than that of a hospital and a less restrictive environment. When insurance covers this form of treatment, it is much less expensive than inpatient hospital care. You would remain at the facility throughout treatment.

## Would Day Treatment Work Better for Me?

This is also known as partial hospitalization. All services of an inpatient facility should be delivered in this program, except you go home to your family at night.

## Is a Halfway House an Option?

A halfway house can be a great transition out of treatment or a low-cost alternative. You would live at the house, work during the day, and attend support groups at night.

## Would Outpatient Care Be Preferable?

You would participate in two to three hours of a program, usually in the evening, while living at home and continuing to work.

# Does the Program Use a Team Approach?

A team approach guarantees that you will have several counselors and therapists working on the case. No one professional bias will be allowed to dictate the type of care delivered.

## How Is the Family Involved?

Treatment that does not involve the entire family is of little value. Problems do not occur in isolation. They are the result of a sick family system that needs to be changed as a whole and not one member at a time. Without family involvement, all of the progress made in the program could be destroyed due to an unhealthy family.

## Will I Get the Personal Attention Required for Effective Treatment?

Some administrators of programs will tell you that individual sessions are not important for quality care. This statement can be due to low staff-to-client ratios that will not allow time for individual sessions. You must find out if the program you are considering offers individual therapy for all clients on an almost-daily basis. If the staff-to-client ratio is low, the quality of care will be low.

## When Can I See the Facility?

No phone call can replace the value of a visit to the facility—seeing firsthand what it looks like and experiencing the feel of the environment.

## Ask Yourself, Is the Treatment Center Well-Maintained?

The first indication of a commitment to quality care is a facility that is clean and well-maintained. It doesn't have to be the newest or the biggest building, but your confidence in the program should be strengthened by the outside appearance and interior maintenance.

## Have I Considered the Wrong Amenities in Choosing a Program?

Some programs will offer horseback riding, swimming, golf, and similar options. These things do not make people well, only comfortable. If there are too many diversions from dealing with the problems at hand, treatment can become a waste of time.

*Stephen Arterburn has spent all of his professional life working in and managing treatment centers for addiction and emotional problems. In 1988 he founded New Life Treatment Centers, which operates programs throughout the United*

*States. He holds degrees from Baylor University and the University of North Texas, as well as two honorary doctorate degrees granted by the California Graduate School of Theology and the University of Honolulu.*

# Additional Resources from Bobb Biehl and Masterplanning Group International

The address is Box 6128, Laguna Niguel, California 92677. Here are the telephone numbers: for orders 1-800-443-1976; for the office 1-714-495-8850; for a fax 1-714-495-0251.

## Please send me the following (free of charge):

☐ Masterplanning Group's resource catalogue (listing books, tapes, seminars)

☐ Consulting information (personal and organizational development)

☐ Speaking information (conferences and executive retreats)

My Name _____

Title _____

Organization _____

Address _____

City _____ State _____ Zip _____

Daytime Telephone ( ) _____

Fax ( ) _____